# TRAILBLAZING

## AMERICA'S FIRST OPENLY GAY
## HIGH SCHOOL COACH

## ERIC ANDERSON

IDENTITY

MANUFACTURED IN THE UNITED STATES OF AMERICA.
COVER DESIGN BY TROY CHERNEY.

THIS TRADE PAPERBACK WAS ORIGINALLY PUBLISHED BY ALYSON
PUBLICATIONS IN MAY 2000 WITH A DIFFERENT SUBTITLE.
SECOND EDITION 2003
IDENTITY PRESS
FOUNTAIN VALLEY, CA. 92708

ISBN 0-9741972-0-3

**LIBRARY OF CONGRESS CATALOGING-IN-PUBLICATION DATA**
    ANDERSON, ERIC, 1968–
        TRAILBLAZING : THE TRUE STORY OF AMERICA'S FIRST OPENLY GAY
    TRACK COACH / ERIC ANDERSON.—1ST ED.
        ISBN 1-55583-524-4
        1. ANDERSON, ERIC, 1968–    . 2. GAY COACHES (ATHLETICS)—
    UNITED STATES—BIOGRAPHY. 3. TRACK—ATHLETICS—UNITED
    STATES. I. TITLE.
    GV1061.14.A53 A3 2000
    796.42'092—DC21                              99-088235
    [B]

COVER PHOTOGRAPHY BY DENNIS CHOTONOVSKY.

# Contents

# INTRODUCTION

In the spring of 1993, at twenty-five years of age, I came out of the closet as an openly gay high school coach in Orange County, California. As one might predict, I was harassed by a homophobic culture that pervades athletics. But while I expected personal difficulties, I had not considered that my heterosexual athletes would also be victimized by homophobic discourse and violence. The story that follows is an account of how my heterosexual teammates came to stand up for me, and sexual minorities in general, as they struggled for equality against a backdrop of overt homophobia, while simultaneously achieving glory on the track. It is an inspiring story of the courage of young allies fighting for a cause they were not born into.

However, one should also remember that the events of this story reflect a historical period. These events would not likely have unfolded the same way today. In fact, my experiences as an openly gay coach inspired me to earn a PhD in sociology, and I now research the nexus of masculinity, homophobia and sport. I am encouraged by my research that shows openly gay male athletes are increasingly accepted by their teammates, and I might encourage readers to visit my website (www.CoachGumby.com) to see what's happening in the world of openly gay athletes, and to look for my upcoming book titled *In the Game: Sport, Homophobia and Gay Male Athletes*.

This book is dedicated first and foremost to my runners – those who are portrayed in the book, and those not. They have offered me support in immeasurable ways, and remain steadfast in their commitment to gay and lesbian causes (they are the heroes of my story). However, the second edition of this text is also dedicated to my partner Grant Tyler Peterson, who (since 1997) has been the support and joy of my life. I am very fortunate to have him there for every new mile I run.

-Eric Anderson

# Chapter One

## The Beginning

*Although some names have been changed, the following events are real.*

In January 1993 the Huntington Beach High School boys' track team, which I coached, organized a community track meet as a fund-raiser. We ended up having more workers than competitors, and rain was nearly the sole occupant of the bleachers lining our ancient brick-dust track. Of the few athletes who showed to compete, one runner caught my eye. His rail-thin body reminded me of a Kenyan runner's; he looked like a champion. He appeared old enough to be in high school, but I didn't recognize him and figured him to be a junior-high runner. Always on the lookout for future athletes, I wanted to find out more. But rules governing our sport prohibited me from speaking to potential athletes until they had graduated from the eighth grade. To circumvent this, I asked one of my runners, Erich Phinizy, to investigate. "Find out his age and where he goes to school," I said. "And tell him about our program."

Erich returned with valuable information. The runner was in junior high and would be attending Huntington Beach next year.

He also informed me that our future runner was of English descent. Erich pointed to the only two people sitting in the bleachers and said, "Those are his parents."

*Damn, not England,* I thought. *They're a bunch of soccer freaks.* I hoped he wouldn't be like a former English runner of mine, who once remarked, "What's the purpose of running if there's no ball to kick along the way?"

Although the soccer coach and I were close friends, we often competed for the same athletes, as soccer players are often runners and vice versa. Each of us ran a quality program, coaching our athletes year-round.

"So, Erich, what's his name?"

"Oh, I didn't get that, Coach. Sorry."

"Don't worry about it."

The possibility of this kid's running for our team excited me, especially since he had come to race the three-mile, an unusually long distance for a 13-year-old. I scanned the entry list and saw, unfortunately, that there were only two other runners in his race. One was a 60-year-old jogger, and the other was Erich. Eager to assess the kid's talent, I asked Erich to pace him. "Run alongside him, encourage him, push him, break the wind for him, see how fast you can get him to run."

Erich agreed.

"Start off slow, though," I warned. "I don't want to discourage the kid."

I fired the gun for the three competitors and watched Erich take the lead. He set the pace and motioned the stick-figure kid to tuck in behind him. Running directly behind another runner is easier, as the wind is broken. Erich paced the kid through what I perceived to be a too-quick first lap. I yelled, "Slow down, Erich!" With 11 of 12 laps remaining, I doubted that the young runner could hold such a furious pace. Erich slowed, but the kid did not, coming up at Erich's side to pass him. Again I yelled, "OK, if that's what he wants, match his pace." One lap after another, Erich led and the kid hung on, running directly behind him. I could tell no one had taught him proper running form. His arms swung awkwardly and inefficiently from side to side, as if he were trying to elbow others around him. He also ran with a large overstride, his feet landing too far in front of his hips, causing a momentary backward thrust with each step, ultimately slowing him down. In addition to poor form, he appeared to be running on 100% effort. His face showed the anguish of a grueling pace. His thin cheeks sucked for oxygen.

I heard the kid's parents cheering for him—"Come on, Dan"—in a distinct English accent. Now knowing the kid's name, I also began to cheer. Dan took over the lead with three laps remaining. He pulled to Erich's side, passed him, and opened a lead. Erich began to falter and would no longer be able to help. I dropped my clipboard and, wearing blue jeans, jumped into the race to take over the job of pacing. I encouraged him. "Stay on me, Dan. Focus on my back," I said, as I ran only a meter in front of him. "You can do it, Dan. Good job, Dan." I paced and encouraged him through the final three laps. He finished in an electrifying time, and though I wasn't supposed to speak to him, I congratulated him anyway. "That was a damn fine race," I said. "I look forward to coaching you next year." I gave him a pat on the back and left to begin the next race.

Although rules prevented me from speaking with Dan, I was allowed to speak with his parents. So after starting the next race, I approached them. Dan's father introduced himself as Stuart and Dan's mother as Liz. Stuart and Liz Gaston. I learned Dan loved to run and was already successful; he was the city's eighth grade two-mile champion. I also learned, to my frustration, that he was interested in joining the soccer team. Already feeling the need to compete for him, I told his parents how much I would like him to join the cross-country and track teams the following school year. I mentioned that I coached the finest distance-running team in the county and tried to sell them on the positive team environment. I spoke to them with the confidence of a seasoned coach—professional, with an air of assurance that the team would be a great place for their son. Internally, however, I worried Dan might choose not to run for me or that his parents might not allow him to run on the team...if they knew the whole truth.

I worried a lot in those days. Although I had coached at Huntington Beach for seven years, I questioned whether I would be allowed to coach the next year at all, despite having developed one of the county's most successful distance-running programs and publishing a best-selling book in the field.

Despite my anxiety, all was well until my secret, the source of my anxiety, was revealed. Now I questioned my future both as an educator and as a coach. Over time I would watch my dreams erode. In the next four years I would experience my greatest struggles, fears, and anger, all while also experiencing incredible joy, pride, and love.

*        *        *

I knew Dan Gaston would be attending Huntington Beach in about eight months, and I was thrilled to know someone talented would be rising through the ranks. Huntington Beach's cross-country team had been formidable since Paul Wood began coaching there in 1968, the year I was born. In fact, Paul was my high school distance coach; I graduated from Huntington in 1986. I began to coach there after graduating and worked as Paul's assistant for four years before he promoted me to head coach.

I hoped Dan would read the local newspapers during the upcoming track season to see just how good the team was and, particularly, how good my individual superstar, Ben Flamm, was. The team I coached was one of the best in the state and the finest in Huntington's history. I wanted Dan to train and race with me year-round instead of choosing soccer or cycling or rugby or whatever the English fancy.

I kept this young runner in the back of my mind until late June.

Each year our athletic director, David VanHoorbeck, visited the local junior high schools to sell students on sports. After each trip he compiled lists of students interested in each sport and gave them to the appropriate coaches. Football always received the most names, while I received the least. After eight years of coaching I had learned to expect anywhere from ten to 15 names and would eventually get half of them to join the team. The others on my list either decided they'd rather be in a "cooler" sport or just didn't like the idea of running 12 miles. Some kids signed up for cross-country thinking it was cross-country skiing. Cross-country skiing in Huntington Beach? During the summer of '93 the athletic director handed me a list of 12 kids interested in running. I scanned the list and spotted the name "Dan." I hoped it was the Dan who had run 12 impressive laps and not some other Dan who might be best suited for shot put.

Even though Dan would be attending Huntington Beach in the fall and had expressed interest in our sport, I couldn't contact him until he graduated from junior high. So I waited until the evening of the eighth grade graduation ceremonies before phoning prospects. I called Dan first, and to my delight it was the same Dan—Dan Gaston.

I assessed new prospects during these initial calls. I'd start off the conversation by making sure students knew they'd be running, not skiing, then I'd probe them for attitudes and behaviors conducive to the rigorous lifestyle a successful distance runner must lead. I listened for responses such as "I love running" or "My parents want me to go into a sport that teaches good values," as opposed to "I figured it would be easier than taking P.E." or "My dad wants me to lose weight." The worst response I ever got was, "Sorry, I can't run. My dad wants me in a real sport."

I called several prospects that night. One of them caught my attention for no reason other than the sheer awkwardness of his last name: *Trueba*—Tony Trueba (pronounced True-aba). It sounded like a perfect name for a top-quality distance runner. Being sufficiently difficult to pronounce, the name was easily screwed up, which of course gave it character. I called Tony to discuss why he wanted to run cross-country.

I couldn't get much out of him at all. The conversation was one-sided and left me wondering if he even recalled signing up for the sport. I did learn he had run in junior high, but if he was good, I didn't know. Months later, however, I would hear from Tony's mom, Cheryl, just how magical that phone call was for him. Tony had returned home from his eighth grade graduation ceremony depressed. He didn't know what high school would hold for him or what he was going to do during the upcoming summer. Quiet and shy, he spent most of his time alone. He had no siblings but had a strong relationship with his parents. His dad, Ricardo, had gotten him into running. In eighth grade Tony had even beaten his dad in a local three-mile race. When I called for Tony that evening, Cheryl later told me he was suddenly elated and eager for the first day's practice.

I awaited the new runners' arrival at 5 o'clock on a characteristically warm Southern California summer evening. This was the first day of practice, June 1993. I was excited to see the new recruits, particularly Dan. I had told them to meet me near my green van, which couldn't be missed, since my license plate read GUMBY. (I have owned the nickname Gumby since sixth grade.)

A gray Volvo station wagon pulled up, and an extremely thin 5-foot-9-inch boy emerged. He sported braces from cheek to cheek and a smattering of age-appropriate zits. It was undeniably Dan, the stick-figure kid who had whizzed around the track eight months earlier. I was surprisingly nervous even though I had coached for years. I wanted to make such an impression on Dan that he would stay in my summer training camp and not participate in the soccer training camp, which began the following week. I introduced myself to him, "I'm Coach Anderson. Welcome to the team."

Several other runners showed that evening, including ones I suspected wouldn't return the following day, ones who acted too cool to be around runners. Distance runners aren't usually the coolest guys on campus, and they are rarely voted homecoming king. The new athletes sat in a circle on the itchy grass and introduced themselves. I asked each to say his name and what school he came from and to list a few of his hobbies. Dan began, "I came from Dwyer Middle School, and I like running, soccer, and cycling." As we moved around the circle, Simon Bhavilai spoke. Simon was a Thai boy with exceptionally large cheeks, oversize glasses, and a huge smile. He didn't possess a runner's build; he was stocky, looking more like a wrestler than a runner. Simon was quiet, perhaps an introvert. Still, he made a positive impression on me when he said, "I'm Simon Bhavilai. I'm not very fast, but I really like to run."

As the introductions continued, Tony Trueba spoke. Trueba, like Dan Gaston, was around 5 foot 9, resembling a puppy dog with large feet he had yet to grow into. He wasn't as thin as Dan; nobody was. By no means did Tony look like a naturally gifted runner. I knew little about him, as he, like Simon, was uncomfortably quiet. What I did not know, or remotely suspect, was that one day those clown feet would sprout wings and fly.

I traditionally give new runners a "Welcome, we need you, we are fun, we are good, there are no cuts, but this is a hard sport" speech. I then tell them about my coaching style and myself. "I graduated from Huntington High in 1986," I began. "As a freshman I was the slowest runner, the one the bus waited for. But I worked hard, and as a sophomore I made the varsity team. By my junior year I was one of the team's best, and during my senior year I broke the school's cross-country record. I've been coaching at Huntington Beach ever since. I still run with the team. Most of the time I run with the top varsity runners because I'm still a competitive runner and need to stay in shape. As your coach, I'll always do what I ask of you, and most of the time I'll do more. If I tell you to run ten miles, I'll run 12. I never yell at my athletes—ever. If I get mad at you, I'll pull you to the side and talk with you privately. You will always know how I feel, and you will never have to guess what I am thinking. If you do a good job, I'll tell you. If you make a mistake, I'll tell you. Gentlemen, there is no hazing on this team. The rest of the team will treat you very well. Finally, if you need to talk, if you have problems, or need anything at all, I have a 24-hour telephone policy. Call anytime. The team is a lot of fun, guys, and all I expect from you is that you treat each other well and be dedicated to the team."

I try to help runners adjust quickly to their new coach and teammates, to feel comfortable with us. I want them to know I care about them and am not overly concerned with winning. A likable personality goes a long way in this sport, as runners usually perform better when they respect their coach. To foster my relationship with the team, I socialize with the runners off the track and show immediate trust in them. I also open up to them about my personal life, my friends, and myself. I had always, however, left out one significant part of my life. I feared they wouldn't stay on the team if they knew the whole truth.

After the initial team meeting we began our workout, a few laps for some and a few miles for others, depending on their level of experience. The first few days of practice are usually uncomfortable for new guys because they don't really know each other. I help introduce them to each other by pairing each freshman with an upperclassman. I paired Dan with Ben Flamm, who had just graduated. He was the best athlete I had ever coached and would be training with us for a few months before flying off to the University of Wisconsin to attend college and run competitively.

As a freshman, Ben possessed a moderate degree of running talent and was a natural leader. A year later he emerged as our team's top sophomore, running fine times. During his junior year Ben won all three team awards: Team Captain, Most Valuable Player, and Most Improved. In addition to his success on the track, Ben was also a talented, mature student. An honors student, he graduated with a grade point average above 4.0. He was also a celebrated member of the debate team and active on the journalism staff. Intellectually, Ben was years ahead of his age—witty, good-natured, and a pleasure to converse with.

A high school runner's year is broken into four parts. First comes the cross-country season in the fall, followed by the winter off-season, in which the runners train but don't race. Track season begins in the spring and ends a month before school lets out. Finally, summer training occurs between the school years. Cross-country runners race three miles, usually in the hills. In track, distance runners can compete in the 800-, 1600-, or 3200-meter races, which correspond closely to the half-mile, the mile, and the two-mile.

Ben finished his senior cross-country season well enough to be offered scholarships to several top-notch colleges. During the month of January, Ben and I traveled together to the Midwest to check out those colleges. It made sense for us to travel together since I was looking at several of the same colleges for my Ph.D.

I wanted to pursue my Ph.D. out of state since I was looking to escape. I wanted to find a place where no one knew me, where there were no preconceived notions of who I was supposed to be or how I was supposed to act. I wanted to step into a new persona. I wanted to flee the life I was living.

Two California boys, accustomed to sun and sand, fantasized the beginnings of a new life in a far-off land. We drove from one college to another, sometimes getting lost in the blinding snow. We prayed we wouldn't run out of gas in the middle of nowhere and be discovered the next day as frozen corpses. We learned things about the Midwest that you don't need to know in California, like how you can't store sodas in the trunk of your car in winter, and if you do, you shouldn't open them inside the car. We also learned how miserable long-distance runs are in the frigid Iowa winter. One night Ben layered up with several shirts, two pairs of sweats, gloves, hats, and scarves, but he still froze during a 12-mile run in air as cold as Newt Gingrich's heart. I tried to help him by driving alongside so the headlights would light his way. I opened the driver's-side window and turned the heater and radio on full blast. Although Ben appreciated this, he swore revenge at my comments: "Jeez, it's nice and warm in this car, Ben" and "God, I'm so hot I think I'm gonna take my jacket off."

We awoke the next morning late for an appointment, left the motel, and discovered our car covered in 18 inches of snow. Worse yet, the windows were completely iced over. I looked at Ben: "How the hell am I supposed to see where I'm driving?" From the side of the door, Ben pulled out a flat plastic device that looked like a back scratcher and said, "I'll save the day." He began to scrape the windows furiously but made no progress at the triple-layer ice. "I'm almost there!" he proclaimed valiantly. I laughed. "Get in the car, you putz." Unable to remove the ice, I drove with my head out the window. My lips turned blue, and I could no longer feel my nose when Ben retaliated with, "Jeez, it's nice and warm in this car, Coach. I think I'll take my jacket off."

We returned from our trip, and Ben began his final track season. He had set lofty goals for himself, including running 9:10 for the two-mile (eight laps). Such a time was about how fast one had to run to qualify for the California state meet in track. Because this is such an extraordinarily difficult task, none of my athletes had ever qualified for the meet. If Ben made it, he would have helped me accomplish one of my four major goals as a high school coach: (1) to advance an athlete to the state meet in track; (2) to advance an athlete to the state meet in cross-country; (3) to win an Orange County cross-country championship title; and (4) to advance a team to the state meet in cross-country.

Although Ben was talented, he was a long way from his 9:10 two-mile goal. His personal record was only 9:42. Nonetheless, throughout the season Ben trained hard and his times began to drop: 9:39…9:32…and in one magical race he dropped to 9:22, a fine time but not nearly fast enough to qualify for the state meet. With four weeks left in the season, Ben and I began to visualize the 9:10 performance he had promised to run. He'd lie on the soft mats of the darkened wrestling room, and I'd call off the exact splits (lap times) he needed to run a 9:10. I guided him through the race and helped him hear, feel, smell, and see the race unfold.

Ben progressed through the championship rounds of competition, but for some reason he ran slower each week. Still, he was fast enough to win the league championship, make it out of prelims and finals, and eventually to the state qualifier. To make it to the state meet, though, he would have to finish in the top five. This normally took a time of about 9:10. But 9:10 was far from the 9:39 he had run the week prior. Thus, many doubted his ability.

At the state qualifiers Ben's strategy was to run the eight laps in the exact splits we had visualized. "Disregard what the others do," I instructed. "Just run your splits. If they surge, you fall back. If they die, you take the lead. Just run your splits and you'll do fine." The gun sounded on a warm May evening, the track lit by a dozen stadium lights and energized by 10,000 fans. Immediately sensing his pace was too fast, Ben moved to the rear of the field. He came through the first lap precisely on time but in last place. He stayed there during the second and third laps but hit his desired splits. His mechanized sense of timing gave me confidence, but part of me worried, seeing him trail so far behind. I had taught Ben to

have patience—that was evident—but    I should have taught
myself the same. I paced alongside the railing, nervously fiddling
with my pen and constantly readjusting my Huntington Beach
cap. During the third lap, trailing by 25 meters, Ben began to reel
the pack in. On the fourth lap he closed the gap to just ten meters.
He hit the mile mark precisely as planned, at 4:35. During the
fifth lap Ben caught the pack and began to work through the runners. Finally, on the sixth lap the other runners began to tire. In a
moment that brought a million goose bumps, Ben took the lead.
He ran exactly as visualized, his pace right on target. I cheered
with all my might, my baritone voice filtering through thousands
of others to find a way to him. Ben could always pick my voice out
of the crowd. "Way to go, Ben!"

With just two laps remaining, however, the pack of runners
behind him began to give chase. Two runners passed him, pushing him back to third place. Fifth place would qualify for the
state meet; he just had to hold off two of the three runners catching him. On the bell lap, with 400 meters remaining, two more
passed him, pushing him back to fifth, the final qualifying spot.
With 200 meters remaining, Ben ran by me on the backstretch.
"Arms, Ben!" I called out. "Drive the arms! He's coming, Ben!
He's coming! Drive, Ben! Drive! Drive!" I yelled with all my
strength, but I couldn't add speed to his legs. Just as the athletes
entered the curve, another runner pulled onto Ben's side. They
headed around the curve, rolled onto the straight-away, and Ben
fell back by only a foot. Energized by the close race, the crowds
cheered wildly. The finish was close, but Ben lost the final qualifying position.

Ben's not qualifying for the meet saddened me, but my disap-
pointment was made easier when the announcements were read:
"And in sixth place, from Huntington Beach, Ben Flamm, with a
time of 9:10.99." He did it! He took 12 seconds off his personal
record. He did exactly as he had said he would. He made me proud.

After Ben's success I longed for another elite athlete, someone to fill his shoes. That someone, I thought, could be Dan. If he would be willing to give up soccer, if I would be permitted to remain as his coach, and if his parents allowed him to be on the team, great things could happen. But that, I realized, was a lot of ifs.

Ben socialized with Dan by driving him home from practice and taking him to events. He convinced Dan of his talent as a runner and tried to turn him away from soccer. "You have a lot of talent, Dan," Ben urged. "You could go far. Four years from now you could be talking to some other freshman, telling him about your state meet race. You could even earn a college scholarship."

*     *     *

As the summer training program progressed, so did my runners. Dan looked like he might be able to shake his inefficient arm jostling, and Tony began to show promise too. On the other hand, Simon proved to be exactly what he said: slow but enthusiastic.

Tony, Dan, and I often ate dinner at the Truebas' home—usually cheeseless pizza. Occasionally, Ricardo would barbecue London broil. I was pleased to learn, during one dinner, that Ricardo was an impressive 4:19 miler in college. Better yet, Tony had an uncle who had placed fifth in the New York City marathon. I decided to take a second look at Tony as a potentially gifted runner. *If he has those genes,* I thought, *I could have* two *talented runners on my hands.*

I asked Dan's father if he had any runners in his family. "No, Coach, sorry," he replied in his thick English accent. "But as a lad in England, I was a national class cyclist, or I at least rode a bike a few times," he chuckled. "Want a beer, Coach?" He knew I didn't drink, but he always asked. Either way, I was pleased to see that Tony and Dan were becoming friends.

In the middle of the summer, Tony showed a glimpse of his potential. I used him as the last resort in a 12-hour relay race, in which each man runs a mile and then passes the baton to a team-mate, who also runs a mile. After all ten runners have gone, the first runner begins again. Once 12 hours have elapsed, the team with the most miles wins. It's a bizarre and grueling race. The high school record, which we wanted to break this year, was held by Fountain Valley, just up the street from Huntington Beach High. Tony was likely to be the team's slowest leg since he had only been running for two months. Dan was in England at the time, so he couldn't run.

Tony donned his first Huntington Beach jersey, and with shoes that looked as if he had just mugged a clown, he ran his first mile in 6:01. He ran each subsequent mile even faster. Tony ran fantastic times for a freshman and helped our team break the all-time record. I realized then that my incoming freshman class had not one potential champion runner on the team but two. With Dan and Tony we had a one-two punch. I dubbed them the Dynamic Duo.

\*       \*       \*

Summer came to a close, and I tearfully said good-bye to my recently graduated seniors. They had been my Dream Team, and they would be missed. Ben was the last to leave. In our final days together we reminisced about his high school days. Ben laughed about his näiveté as a freshman, recalling how he once thought wearing ankle weights would help him run faster. We also talked about how good the Dynamic Duo could someday be. Ben was the only one who knew everything I was going through, the only one who knew my secret; he understood that if Dan and Tony learned the truth about their coach and quit the team, it would kill me. Losing my most promising runners to prejudice would destroy my spirits. The question hovered over our conversations. I could tell Ben wanted to ask how I felt about it but couldn't bring himself to discuss it, as if talking about it would somehow jinx the outcome.

Ben and I had each come to a different conclusion from our trip to the Midwest. He chose to pursue his dreams at the University of Wisconsin, one of the top three cross-country schools in the nation, while my visit left me homesick. I missed my team, the sun, and the dazzling blue waters of the Pacific Ocean. I realized escape couldn't solve what plagued me. I decided to return home and face the reality of my life.

Ben's departure for college came too soon. I drove him to the airport, my eyes growing misty long before we entered the terminal. With the announcement "Final boarding call for Flight 923," I placed Ben's bag on the floor, opened my arms, and hugged him, squeezing hard. Ben said, "I'll miss you, Coach." Through sodden eyes, I looked at him and offered, "Make me proud, Ben." I turned and walked a few strides, then stopped and looked over my shoulder, catching a final glimpse of him entering the boarding tunnel. He saw me and waved good-bye, then turned and boarded the plane.

I returned from that tearful good-bye to a new season and the excitement of my talented freshman runners. How fast could they run? How far would they go? I couldn't wait to find out.

I had only one fear: Would they care, would they quit, if they knew I was gay?

# Chapter Two

## Temperament of the Times

I have always known that I am gay. Since I was 6 years old, I found boys cute and wanted to be close to them. First it was Pat, my friend from across the street. One day when his mom wasn't home, we took a shower together. I remember being excited, but I didn't understand why. When I was 8, I went to see *Star Wars* on opening day. Before the curtain rose, I spotted a boy a few aisles down and a couple of seats over. My eyes fixed on him. I was envious of his friend sitting next to him. I'd had similar feelings before, for Pat and other boys. I realized I was staring at him for an unacceptable period of time. Aware that my actions could alert others to my secret desires, I blurted an excuse. "Mom," I said, "I want my hair cut like his." I already knew how to hide my true identity. Although I didn't know my actions had a label, I was "passing" at age 8.

Not only did I know I was gay, but I also understood that society condemned it. Without having gone through puberty, and therefore lacking real sexual desire, I decided to go through life hiding my "problem." I neither spoke about it nor asked any questions. On the way to school one morning, however, my mother and I heard a debate on the radio about whether gays should be permitted to teach. Today I recognize this debate as the Briggs initiative, supported by the monstrous homophobe Anita Bryant. I asked my mother what the fuss was about. She said, "There's a group of people who don't want gay teachers." I asked, "Why not?" She replied, "I don't know, Eric. The only thing that should matter is how good a teacher is." Her logic made sense to me.

I never heard the outcome of that initiative. Even in my adult years I was afraid to ask. Asking would tip people off, wouldn't it? I assumed gays weren't permitted to teach, since I never knew a gay teacher, nor had I heard the issue discussed after the Briggs initiative debate. Yet, all this was irrelevant, I told myself, since I wasn't about to reveal my secret to anyone.

At age 12 I grew attracted to my best friend, Sean. I wanted to be around him whenever I could and enjoyed wrestling with him on the living room carpet. I especially liked to pin him down and lie on top of him to keep him down. Wrestling and running were the only physical activities at which I excelled. I wasn't very athletic back then; actually, I was a motor moron. To make matters worse, I never learned the rules and practices of formal sport. By the time I was old enough to realize I didn't know how to play baseball, football, or basketball, I was too embarrassed to ask my friends or father to show me.

My dad wasn't much of a jock either, so teaching me about sports wasn't a high priority. He liked UCLA football because he had earned his bachelor's degree there before landing a job in the aerospace industry, but that was the extent of his athletic interest. Both Mom and Dad were academically, not athletically, minded. When I was 5 my parents decided they both wanted better careers than the aerospace industry offered, so they continued working full-time in the day and attended law school by night. When I was 9 they graduated from law school in the top of their class. In fact, my mother graduated summa cum laude, with the highest grade point average in the school's history. Soon after, an insurance firm hired my father, and my mother took a job with the public defender's office. She then ran for, and won, judgeship in 1984 when I was 16. Eventually, she worked her way up to the position of presiding judge.

Having intelligent parents was valuable, even if they didn't prioritize sports. Nonetheless, it would have been nice to know how to play the games so that I wouldn't have been socially ostracized. When a kid fails in the classroom, his failure is usually known only to the student, the teacher, and the parents. When a kid fails on the athletic field, he fails publicly.

I once hit a fly ball to center field during a junior high baseball game, and although the ball was caught, I still ran the bases. I thought the object of the game was to get back to home plate before the ball did. I ran the bases furiously, landed on home plate, and victoriously threw my hands into the air to celebrate my scored run. Imagine my embarrassment when I learned I was out four bases ago.

Volleyball was no different. My grade-school gym teacher was similar to most, in that he didn't actually *teach* physical education— he simply rolled a ball out to the kids and let them go at it. I couldn't figure out how the other kids could serve with such accuracy and feel none of the pain I experienced. My wrist grew red after each serve, and I had no control over the ball's direction. I looked goofy hitting the ball with all my might and watching it spin out of control only a few feet ahead of me. Not until age 21 did I learn you're supposed to hit the ball with the heel of the hand, not your wrist.

The nickname Gumby also came as the result of a sporting folly, during a sixth grade football game. At the moment of kick-off I stood with my arms folded over my chest, as a biplane flying overhead diverted my attention. Not realizing the ball had been kicked and the opposing players were charging, I stood oblivious yet looked ready to block. One of the larger players hit me hard, launching me backward through the air. I landed on my butt, to the uproarious laughter of everyone on the field. One of my friends said I looked like Gumby flying through the air. The name was, of course, meant to ostracize me, and for a couple of years it did just that. Gumby, however, was a name not easily forgotten, and before long, it made me popular, and I grew to like it.

Sean left after seventh grade, and I found a new best friend in Chris. He liked to spend the night at my house because we could sneak *Playboy* magazines from my father's stack in the closet. I pretended to be interested in the photos but wasn't attracted to the rounder stomachs and full breasts that women possessed. After Chris fell asleep, I'd lie next to him, longing to lie on top of him.

During eighth grade I spent the night with a friend named Tommy. He was moving to Alaska the next day, and this was a farewell event. We were alone in his room when he jokingly called me a name. I retaliated by attacking him, and a wrestling match broke out. After rolling around with him, I finally pinned him. Exhausted, he stopped fighting. Breathing hard, I held his arms down as I sat on his midsection. I made eye contact, the kind that suggests an impending kiss. Tommy looked to me and said in an affirming voice, "What are you going to do, kiss me?" I wanted to badly. Now I look back and realize that his tone of voice, his eye contact, his inviting only me to spend the night, all meant that he did too. But I didn't kiss him and have regretted it ever since.

After graduating from the eighth grade, I vacationed on a cruise ship with my parents in the Caribbean. On board, I met an adorable boy named Lance. Mournfully, Lance was straight, the kind of guy that starts hanging photos of girls in his room at age 6. We stood on an aft deck late one night, while a warm tropical sea breeze lifted Lance's hair, making him look sexy. He stood near the rail, gazing at the moonbeams dazzling in the rippling waters below. The bright moon lit his boyish face, and I positioned myself to take in the splendor of the ocean along with his appealing physique. Overcome with desire, I soon discovered I was not alone in my thoughts of romance. Lance turned to me and said, "It sure would be a great night to be with a girl, wouldn't it?"

Disappointed but still bathed in hope, I replied, "It doesn't have to be with a girl." The words shocked me. Had I said that? Apprehensively, I awaited his response.

"What?! You're not gay, are you?"

Hoping I was not alone in this passion, I didn't answer; I only chuckled. Lance barked, "Just say no!" Crushed, I blurted, "Hell, no! I just thought it was funny you would ask." The next week, I became a freshman at Huntington Beach High School.

A paranoid fear of being thought gay and feeling inferior to other boys were hallmarks of my freshman year—undoubtedly the worst year of my life. I was frustrated, scared, intimidated, and alone in my attraction to boys. These feelings, combined with my rampant teenage libido, created a recipe for constant strife. P.E. class was particularly painful. Not only was I unschooled in athletics, but also the locker room presented real problems. I dreaded changing clothes for fear of getting an erection. Once the bell sounded I would sprint from math class to the locker room, trying to be one of the first to change. I could never get there first, though, because my math class was on the other side of campus. As soon as I entered and saw the half-naked bodies, I would grow hard. I tried not to look, but the desire was strong. I learned to carry my bag in front of me, to hide my erection, and to change quickly while facing the lockers. When P.E. was over and the teacher dismissed us, I would sprint to the locker room under the guise of proving my "superior speed." In reality, I was trying to beat the other guys there so I could change before they arrived. Erection protection, I called it.

My P.E. class had one redeeming value: the opening warm-up lap. I always raced with a guy named Chris, who was also a fast runner. Some days I'd win, and some days he would. Perhaps my erection-protection training had made a decent runner out of me. Chris and I struck up a friendship, and we began to hang out after school. I invited him on a weekend camping trip in the mountains with my father and me. That night, after a day of hiking and fishing, we returned to our two-man tent. Although we were in separate sleeping bags, we were nestled close, and I could feel the warmth of his body. I strategically moved a leg closer, under the guise of changing positions for comfort. I hoped he would return my subtle maneuvers with advances of his own. As the evening grew on, I grew braver. Under the pretense of being asleep, I rolled over and put my arm around him. He awoke, took my arm off, and rolled away. Afterward, I feared he knew I was gay. Although he mentioned nothing of it the next morning, I envisioned him returning to P.E. to tell the whole class.

As I walked into the locker room Monday morning, I read a sign: FRESHMAN BOYS WANTED FOR CROSS-COUNTRY. SEE COACH WOOD AT THE TRACK DURING SIXTH PERIOD. *Cross-country? That's running,* I thought. *Hell, I can do that.* It would be my ticket out of my P.E. class, and I wouldn't have to face Chris.

I walked onto the track to see a group of older boys standing around—and screwing around—while an old man with thinning white hair took roll. He was professional looking with his gray briefcase and a jacket with H.B. CROSS-COUNTRY stenciled on one side, and COACH WOOD on the other. I told him I was thinking about running for the team. He welcomed me and pointed me to the freshman row. I met the other athletes and tried to imitate their stretches. Then we ran two miles to our local park. When we arrived, Coach Wood, who ran with us, assigned the workout. I was in shock; we had just run two miles to the park, were going to run six more, and then run the two miles home. Knowing I could not handle this, I told Coach Wood, "I need to leave, so I can catch my 3:30 bus." He asked if I knew the way home, and I said yes. I left the park, running at first, then walking once I was out of sight. I walked until I was lost. I found a pay phone, called my father, and asked him how to get back to the high school.

That night Coach Wood phoned to see if I wanted to run. I told him I wasn't sure since I was on the school's debate team and didn't know if I'd have time. He said, "Well, if you can't handle it, I'll understand." *Who is he to tell me I can't handle it?* I thought. I told him to hang on while I asked my parents. I set the phone down and asked myself if I really wanted to do this. "My mom says it's OK."

I grew to like Coach Wood. He was old, conservative, and yelled a lot, but he gave me time and attention. He spoke with the remnants of an accent he acquired from growing up in Oklahoma. And he was full of what I call Woodisms, witty sayings to describe people and situations: "If you had one more brain cell...you'd have one." "You couldn't run that fast off a cliff." That sort of thing.

One of my favorite freshman memories was competing against Coach Wood in a 100-meter race. The finish was close, and today we each claim to be the victor. I thought he ran pretty well for an old guy. Several weeks later he had a disc removed from his back. He never ran again and has yet to admit defeat to me. I never asked Coach Wood how he felt about gay people. It didn't really matter because it seemed everyone hated them.

Things improved during my sophomore year. Running raised my self-esteem, and I began to excel at it. This, combined with improved physical looks when my braces came off, bolstered my confidence. Girls began to take interest in me, though I had no interest in them. Still, I did have my first girlfriend my sophomore year. She ran for the girls' team, and I went over to her house because I was interested in her brother. She and I began to date, but when things progressed to where I found myself making out with her in my car, I created a reason why I no longer liked her and stopped calling her.

Expectations of dating were high during my junior year. A somewhat popular and decent-looking guy is expected to date. Should I avoid the school dances or should I ask a girl to attend with me? Most of the time I opted for avoidance, giving excuses such as, "I don't want to be out late before my race" or "I have to work." My friends attended and danced with their dates vertically during the event, and horizontally after. This produced a great deal of jealousy on my part, especially when it came to Brian.

Brian was a year younger than I was. We possessed similar running ability and often trained together. Brian was gorgeous, his slender body distinctly defined with barely any body fat. His soft, curly blond-red hair and room-warming smile enhanced his looks. My sexual desire for Brian was stronger than it had been, or has ever been, for any other man.

Thus far, the story of my dating life had been a broken record. I fell in love with guys who could no more return my love than I could that of a woman. Brian, unfortunately, was no different. Although I desired him more than life itself, I received no signs of mutual feelings. I picked him up for school every morning and dropped him off at home after. I bought him gifts and invited him on trips. I tried everything to be close to him. Perhaps I was trying to buy his love. All my efforts, of course, were to no avail. When Brian began dating women, I grew intensely jealous. We worked together at a movie theater, and when an attractive girl came in, Brian would try to get her phone number. I took great delight in his failures and great pain in his successes.

Under the intoxication of alcohol or passion, on so many desperate occasions, I longed to utter the words "I am gay." At one time, the attempt made it as far as my trembling hand. I scrawled *I am gay* on a piece of paper. In fright, that same hand soon tore the proclamation into unrecognizable pieces then burned them.

As desperately as I desired to speak my truth, I was terrified I would actually do it. I also wondered if my actions had, in some way, sent clues to others about what I was harboring. Over and over I asked myself, Did I look at that guy too long? Did I look at that girl long enough? Did I say "he" instead of "she"? Mostly I feared that my friends suspected. A gay man's fear of being discovered is similar to that of a convict's on the run: He keeps careful track of his own words, of where he goes, of what others know. I kept my eyes straight ahead in the locker room, talked about girls, and even swiveled my head as I drove past them, with one arm rested in butch fashion on the opposite seat back. I dated them, got close to them, and made out with them, but I never enjoyed them.

I was in high school during the extreme AIDS phobia and homophobia that characterized the mid 1980s. At that time homosexuality was detestable; there was nothing worse. Teachers, fine teachers, spoke of putting gays on islands—like lepers—to "protect the rest of us." "They're going to kill us all," said one teacher whom I had held in high esteem. The tyranny was everywhere, including my own home. My older brother said, "Fags should be shot!"

My fiery jealousy of Brian's dating, the anguish of being without him, the paranoia of being discovered, the frustration of my desire, and the solitude I felt evoked thoughts of suicide. I didn't know a single gay person and had tried for years to change my desires. I attempted to masturbate while visualizing the opposite sex, only to discover that the closer to orgasm I grew, the more the women looked like Brian. I even appealed to God for a cure. Alone, and in despair, suicide seemed the only answer.

I dropped Brian off late one night after returning from a party where he had successfully scored the number of yet another girl. In an agitated state of jealousy and frustration, I accelerated my Camaro to 100 miles per hour down a one-mile stretch of road that was dark, deserted, and straight. The air was black with a dense fog that rolled off the coast. At the end of the mile stretch was a sharp 90-degree left-hand turn and a metal railing to prevent cars from running off the road and over the adjacent cliff. A flashing red light signaled the stop but was dimmed by a thick blanket of late-night fog. I would wait for the first flash of visible red before hitting the brakes. It was a gamble as to whether the light would shine at a sufficient stopping distance before the road's end. I maintained my speed and steered straight toward the cliff.

Finally, light penetrated the fog and I hit the brakes. My tires squealed, and the car rocked and swayed from side to side as it decelerated. I swung the car to the left, and the momentum pulled me into a sideways skid, directing the car off the road and into the thick dirt. Dust gathered in the air, mixing with the fog. The car stopped. I accelerated again, spinning the tires and spewing more blankets of dirt, and headed toward the next street signal. I tightened my jaw and clenched my hands on the steering wheel as I pressed the pedal to the floor. My pulse raced with the engine as I attempted to see what lay before me in the fog. I had no intention of stopping at the light if it turned red. I waited for a color to materialize through the fog.

Red. It's red.

Adrenaline surged through me and sweat streamed down my forehead as I ran the light. I emerged unscathed on the other side. I slowed my Camaro and began a deep cry. Tears clouded my vision as badly as the fog had a few moments earlier. I pulled the car into a neighborhood and chose a dark place to park. As I cried, I longed for someone to find me, to rescue me.

If someone had just tapped on my window, shown compassion, and asked what was troubling me, I would have confessed my secret and melted into his arms. Weeping, I sat awaiting my savior. The night grew colder, the windows fogged over, and I began to realize no guardian angel would rescue me. I was, as before, alone. I drove home to a society colder than the evening's air.

I began to drink at weekend parties, where I'd try to muster the courage necessary to speak my truth, or even make a pass at a guy. If I were rejected, I figured I could blame it on the influence of alcohol. But I never drank enough to tell someone I was gay. Inebriated, I once competed in a contest to see who could jump off the highest step on a stairway. Someone would go first, and then the next guy would have to either jump a step farther or lose by chickening out. I'm not sure how many steps the guy in front of me cleared, but I jumped to a crash landing on my knees.

A few days later in health class, my teacher, Mr. Moore, talked about alcohol abuse. Mr. Moore was an thin, gray-haired elderly man who walked with a long loping stride and had an engaging smile and kind eyes. Although he was old, he could relate to teenagers, and I valued his lessons. He made a statement regarding alcohol that changed my life. "I don't really believe in alcoholism as something to define," he said, "It's too hard to say when someone is or isn't an alcoholic. I like the term *problem drinker*. Anytime alcohol causes a problem in your life, you are a problem drinker." His comments set me to thinking about what I had done on the stairs. Nearly ruining my running career was certainly a problem, and I vowed to never drink again. I have remained a nondrinker ever since.

Mr. Moore's health class was the most influential class I ever took. He inspired me, and I looked to him as a mentor. He knew how to help me, never judged, and always provided kind words and good insight. His liberal attitudes and loving nature influenced me so much that I began spending my lunch periods with him.

Mr. Moore said something else that profoundly affected me. He was progressive, as he talked about homosexuality in his health class and made it clear that he had no problems with it. He viewed homosexuality as just another facet of human sexuality and said, "We Americans get worked up over nothing." His most powerful statement, however, came when he said, "You don't truly know whether you're gay until you're 25." I don't think Mr. Moore actually believed that. Rather, I believe the statement was designed for me. I think he knew I was gay all along. He had us keep journals that only he read, and mine all but screamed, "I'm gay!" Almost every entry focused on Brian. Although I never stated my love for Brian directly, an educated man could have easily detected it.

His statement allowed me to put off dealing with my sexuality. It gave me a kind of hope. But it also led me to try to change my sexuality, believing I had until I was 25. Futilely, I again attempted to fantasize about women while masturbating. I repeated "I am straight" affirmations ten times a day. Although Mr. Moore both helped and hindered my mental health as a gay boy, overall he inspired and supported me to the highest degree. In fact, I was so inspired that I decided to become an influential and loving health teacher just like him.

My efforts to convert to heterosexuality proved worthless, and during my senior year my affection for Brian grew stronger than ever. By now I had learned to pass as heterosexual like a professional. I had trained myself not to look at guys, and I spoke of women in the same heterosexual way as my friends. At least I thought I did.

I saw life in different shades my senior year. I grew more competitive as a runner, became our school newspaper photographer, and quit my job at the movie theater. My self-esteem improved, and I felt confident I could speak to, lead, and influence others. As a senior, there were no elders to feel inferior to, and I took on the position of team captain with pride. Most importantly, I began to adapt to my situation. I realized my sexuality was permanent and unchangeable. I ceased torturing myself by trying to convert to heterosexuality. I allowed myself the freedom to enjoy fantasizing about Brian or Chris or whoever the hell else I desired. I replaced my affirmations of heterosexuality with affirmations about distance running. I eased up on myself and allowed myself to simply be me. By giving in, I was happier.

As a freshman on my college team at California State University, Long Beach, I was at the bottom rung once again. No longer team leader, I was barely a member of the varsity squad. Other runners intimidated and hazed me. It was normal to have a girlfriend, have sex, and share the details with the rest of the guys. I had no girlfriend and no sex to report. My level of intimidation grew to the point where I was afraid to attend practice or the team's social events, which often involved drinking. One night my fellow teammate and roommate asked me why I was being such a stick in the mud. "My goals, Mark, are to be a dynamic health teacher and cross-country coach. I am here to accomplish that, not to drink beer and run laps naked." In reality, I was afraid of being too social with the guys because they might figure me out.

Just as in P.E. my freshman year of high school, I needed out. So I returned to Huntington Beach as a part-time coach. Coaching helped me to feel worthy again. I was also free of intimidation. Coach Wood offered to hire me as his assistant, and I accepted. I was 18.

I dreamed of being a coach as seasoned as Coach Wood and a health teacher as influential as Mr. Moore. I set myself on the path of being a superb distance coach by doing just that: coaching. To be a health teacher, however, I had to make an academic move. Acquiring a California teaching credential in health science required I have a minimum grade point average of 3.2. Upon completing my freshman year of college, I had only a 2.1. Simple math, at which I was not so good, told me I needed to improve significantly over the next few years. One professor, whose wisdom I have not forgotten, but whose name I have, changed my life with one question. After taking roll in a half-full class, he raised his wire-rimmed glasses and asked, "People, why do you let us take your money?" The thought was revolutionary to me: If I'm paying to go to school, I should show up to gain benefit from what I have paid for. With that, I devoted myself to my studies. My grades rose, and by the end of my sophomore year, I was a 3.8 student.

I learned to love the acquisition of knowledge, and I began to read books about running, health, psychology, and the hard sciences. I spent my days studying, writing, and coaching. These diversions were good for me because they not only gave me confidence and knowledge but also provided an excuse for not dating.

Being busy works well as an excuse for not dating, but part of the art of passing involves learning *when* to date. For maximum visibility, it is considerably smarter to bring a date to a party or family function than it is to take a girl out alone. As a junior in college, I pulled off the highest grade possible in "Passing 101." I sat as Bachelor Number 1 on the nationally televised show *The Dating*

*Game*. Killing two birds with one stone was nothing; I shot down a whole flock. Not only did I bring my team to watch the taping, but my mother also informed all the relatives, including some I never knew I had. I "lost" the date in the end (which, I guess, is to say I really "won"). What still irks me, however, was that I should have won. The question "When don't you like to kiss a girl?" was asked, and although I wanted to say "Always," I responded, "When I'm in the beautiful blue waters of the Caribbean Ocean scuba diving. It just makes it hard to breathe." OK, maybe it's not the greatest impromptu answer, but I think it's better than the winning answer: "When she has frog lips." All was not lost, though, as I received a box of floor tile and a case of bubble gum as consolation prizes.

When I was 21 I met a boy named Larry who lived in my apartment complex. Larry was a senior in high school, sort of a runner, and impressively cute. He was also father to a host of problems: drugs, divorced parents, girl problems, insecurities, and a hatred of school. I became his confidant. Larry frequented my condo and talked about his various problems. One day he came for help with an English assignment. I sat at my desk, answering his questions while he lay on my bed munching Doritos. He put down his paper and said, "I want to talk to you about something."

"Sure. What is it?" I asked.

"I like guys."

Fear shot through me. My hands began to tremble as I heard, for the first time, the words I had longed to utter. Moreover, they were proclaimed not by me but by another. Larry said what I never could. My shaking grew worse as I realized the significance of the situation. The need to announce my truth fought with fear. I wanted to let go of my secret, but I couldn't say anything comprehensible; I just mumbled. My shaking grew so violent that I began to convulse. I tried to speak but could not. My tongue couldn't say what my body shouted, betraying me with quivering knees and trembling hands. Finally, my lips broke their hold. "I, uh, I, uh, em, I do too."

I don't really know if all my words were audible; my most prominent memory is that of incredible shaking. Nonetheless, I had said it. And in that most awkward moment, both of us having revealed our true selves, we just sat. We didn't know what to do or say. I didn't speak or move. I just shook. "I…I have to go," Larry said. He gathered his stuff and quickly ran out the door, leaving me still shaking in my seat.

Larry knocked on my door a few days later. Although nervous, I was elated to see him. "Hi, Larry. What's up?" I closed the door behind him. Larry was direct and quick: "Do you want to have sex?" Again, I began to shake. "Uh…what?…OK…yes, yes." Larry had it all planned out. He produced a key to the place of a friend who was out of town for the weekend. "No one can walk in on us," he said. (I had two homophobic roommates, so my place was out of the question.)

When we got to his friend's apartment, we closed the door, and—my God—I was scared. Larry turned on some music and asked, "Do you like it?" I didn't but replied, "Yeah, it's great." He came over to me, and we looked at each other oddly. We slowly maneuvered to kiss, our heads going to the same side at first. Then I pressed my lips against his. Larry draped his arms around me and lowered me to the carpet below.

When my first same-sex experience was over, I regretted it. I left with an ill feeling. Perhaps I was not gay. I mean, if I didn't enjoy the sex, didn't that mean I wasn't gay? I certainly enjoyed the orgasm, but I didn't enjoy kissing Larry. I hated the smell his saliva made on my skin, and I was left with a bad taste in my mouth. More than that, I was afraid others would find out. Whenever I saw him in the common areas of the building, I was too busy to talk; Larry quit coming over.

Several months later Larry stopped by and told me he was moving. After our experience he came out rapidly. He had met several guys, and his father had caught him having sex with one of them. His dad had decided to move him to a more "Christian" atmosphere than Long Beach, and I never found out where. I haven't heard from him since. The experience scared me, and I drove myself back into the closet. I even began to try to convert myself again.

A year later I graduated with a bachelor's degree in health science, and after a semester of graduate work, I began student teaching at Fountain Valley High School. My advisor was Mike Hennigan. In his early 50s, he was also the athletic director and football coach. Mike was the stereotypical football coach, and I learned that I was given the assignment not because he could teach me something about health but because I could provide him with more time to work on his football plays. I easily, perhaps foolishly, labeled Mike a dumb jock. To add to my insecurity, I found a Bible in his desk drawer. I considered this a warning from up high not to discuss with him my plans of teaching gay issues, masturbation, or any other controversial sexual topics. Fortunately, he only sat in on my class a few times. I feared if he heard some of the liberal things I said, I would be reprimanded, so I planned benign activities for the days he observed me.

I met another student teacher during my internship at Fountain Valley. Michelle taught English and was undeniably attractive. We hit it off as friends, and I soon found myself visiting her at her home. Lying on her bed, we talked late one night. We discussed life, sex, music, movies, and other matters relevant to 22-year-olds. The topic of sex emerged more frequently than others, and somewhere along the line I admitted to still being a virgin. Michelle had thought I was the master of sex, as she had sat in on my health class when we discussed it. Amazed that I hadn't actually engaged in it, she asked if I would like to have sex with her. I didn't really want to but figured it would be hard to talk my way out of it. "OK, sure," I said. She began to undress. I grew hard, but when she stood naked before me, her stomach and chest were too round, too female.

I suppose the sex was more interesting than watching television, but I had liked it a lot more with Larry, even though my experience with him had not been great. The evening did, however, give me bragging rights. I arrived home at 3 o'clock in the morning, making sufficient noise to wake my roommates. They knew I was at Michelle's house, and the night would serve as a useful weapon against any suspicions they might have had about my sexuality.

I ended my student teaching at Fountain Valley and in the process earned my teaching credential. The market for health teachers was slim, so I took a job as the resident substitute at Huntington Beach High School. No longer in school, I was loaded with spare time. I taught in the morning, coached in the afternoon, and had absolutely nothing to do in the evening. I wondered what excuse I would now find for not dating. Therefore, I could hardly say no when a runner of mine suggested setting me up with the older sister of a girl he was dating. I was in my early 20s, thought I could conceal my secret forever, and figured I would someday have to marry. Here was an opportunity. The girl came complete with a small child too—the ready-made family. So I began to date her.

I was miserable and could only stretch the lie a few weeks. I broke up with her. And I worried. If I could not live a heterosexual lie more than a few weeks, how was I going to live one for a lifetime?

I fell back to a tried-and-true solution. As an excuse for not dating, I would go back to school at night. I continued to teach during the day, coach in the afternoons, and attend school at night. Initially, I enrolled in a marriage, family, and child counselor program at Cal State Long Beach. But I was only a month into my schooling when I received terrible news.

A security guard ran frantically to the track. "Is Eric Anderson here?"

"I'm Eric. What's up?"

"You have an emergency phone call waiting for you in the office. Something is wrong with your father."

I rushed to the phone to hear the voice of my mother's secretary. "Eric, your father has been taken to St. Mary's in Long Beach. Your mom wants you there right away."

"I'm on my way."

I hung up, ran to Coach Wood for directions, and made my way there. I knew my father's smoking, drinking, stress, and lack of exercise were going to catch up with him sooner or later. I entered the hospital and approached the information desk. "I'm Eric Anderson. I was told my father is here," I said. The receptionist asked me to hold on. She picked up the phone and said, "Eric Anderson is here." With that, a priest walked down the hallway.

My father died of a sudden and massive coronary heart attack at age 55. He would never know I was gay, never know of my accomplishments, and will never read this book.

Depressed, I dropped out of school. I continued my job as the resident substitute and decided to return to school the next year, after I received money from my father's life insurance policy. I was determined to use the money to support myself while I went back to school to earn a master's degree in sport psychology. I'm certain my father would be happy to know I used the money to further my education.

Again I enrolled at Cal State Long Beach, and over the next two years I studied, wrote two books, produced great teams, and chased my dreams. The only thing holding me back from happiness was my hidden sexuality.

My body soon began to rebel. I developed migraine headaches every other week, then weekly, then twice a week. Eventually, a migraine hit almost every day. Then came stomach pains and symptoms of an ulcer. I didn't want to see a doctor because I feared he might figure out what was causing it. Next came a painful sciatic nerve condition. I, the health teacher and runner, was ailing.

I suffered with these symptoms for a year and a half. At age 25—the age Mr. Moore had said you don't know you are truly gay until you have reached—I still was suffering. To all others, my life appeared to be going quite well. I was producing my thesis to complete my master's degree, I had placed a down payment on a house, and I had a contract to publish my first book, *Training Games*. I was also coaching the sensational Ben Flamm. I should have been on top of the world. Instead, I was miserable. I had returned from my Midwest trip with Ben a few months earlier, knowing it was time to come out of the closet.

In April 1993, during Ben's senior year, I walked by the front doors of a gay resource center. This required all the courage I could muster. I first flew past the doors at a speed of Mach 3, later returning for a second pass at half the speed. Finally, after making failed attempts over several days, I stepped inside. Spotting a rack of pamphlets, I quickly turned my back to a group of guys sitting on a couch and randomly selected a pamphlet. Terrified, I exited as fast as I could, my heart pounding rapidly. I sped away, looking around to make sure no one saw me. Finally, far away from the center, I stopped and looked at the pamphlet I had chosen: "Women's Health."

I saw something else during my microsecond adventure to the gay resource room: the gorgeous blue eyes of a man in his early 20s who worked in the resource center. Those sparkling eyes inspired me to return home and call the center. Undoubtedly, the sweet voice that answered the center's phone belonged to those eyes. "Hello. What time is your next support meeting?" I managed to ask.

The next meeting happened to be that evening. I hung up the phone, dialed a friend's number, and hung up before he could answer, ensuring if a roommate hit redial, it wouldn't be met with, "Gay resource center." I sat on the corner of my bed and summoned a dozen excuses for not attending, but a set of blue eyes compelled me to go. So I did.

Under the cover of darkness, I walked into the gay resource center again. I passed the pamphlets and headed straight for the couch away from the window. People began introducing themselves, and eventually the owner of those blue eyes introduced himself as David. I experienced the most terrifying sense of liberation at that meeting: I was afraid someone would walk in and see me; on the other hand, I hoped someone would.

That taste of freedom, so sweet, so feared, beckoned me again. Like an addict, I secretly craved the high. I returned to the meeting the next week and soon found the courage to stop by during the middle of the day. I began to hang out with David. I sleuthed around the gay community with David as my guide. He introduced me to gay culture and hangouts and answered the questions that go along with most everyone's coming out. Finally, with David, I had sex I truly enjoyed. Our relationship continued to grow, and one night David stayed over. I snuck him into my room late at night, and he left early the next morning.

A few weeks later I attended, with 25,000 of the friendliest people, the Long Beach gay pride parade and festival. I marched with conviction down a public street. My first boyfriend and I walked freely, with thousands of others who loved me for who I was. I marveled at the number of older men, African-Americans, Asians, Mexicans, lesbians, transvestites, and people far younger than I. I loved the T-shirts that stated I'M NOT GAY, BUT MY BOYFRIEND IS or NOBODY KNOWS I'M GAY.

David introduced me to new friends—and many of his old boyfriends too. "That one has a big dick," he'd say. "That one was an asshole." "That one this, and that one that." I understood the situation. I was not a romantic interest to David. I was a fuck and nothing more.

At age 25 I was suffering from my first broken heart. With girls, I had always hoped to be dumped. If they didn't dump me, I'd find a reason to end it. I now knew the pain of puppy love. I was ashamed of my ignorance and hurt by my loss, but mostly I was grieving because I couldn't share my loss with anyone. Of all the people whose lives I had touched—my friends, family, and team— surely I deserved someone with whom to discuss my sorrow. For all the consoling I had done for others, I deserved to be consoled myself. But how could I tell someone what I was feeling, what my pain was about, without coming out?

With that thought, I found my answer and my freedom. To be free, to be me, and to be happy, I had to come out. I decided to call my best friend, Jeff. He had always supported me, had always been there when I needed him. Jeff also supported gays wholeheartedly. He just didn't know he'd been supporting me. Many of the problems I had brought to Jeff were half problems, parts of the whole, never fully assembled. I remember talking to Jeff as a junior in high school, explaining to him how I was mad at Brian, how I felt Brian was using me. Jeff tried to convince me that I deserved more. But he didn't know I was in love with Brian and pained over not being able to say how I felt. Still, Jeff was there for me. I decided to tell him first.

I paced by the phone for an hour as I tried to work up the courage to call. I finally stopped the tears and dialed. I misdialed twice before getting the number correct. "Jeff, I need to talk to you," I said calmly. Then it hit. Tears of more than 20 years of worry and fear began to flow, releasing my thoughts of suicide, loneliness, and insecurity.

"Jesus, Eric. What's wrong?"

All I could do was cry.

"Where are you?"

"Home."

"I'll be right there."

"No," I said. "Meet me in the parking lot."

"I'll be there as fast as I can, Eric."

Jeff arrived to find me sitting in my car shaking, crying, and terrified. I felt like a deer trapped in the sights of a hunter's gun. I was about to open myself up to be fired at by a heterosexist society. Nonetheless, years of pent-up fear were now willing to be heard. I cried, unable to speak, as Jeff waited for over half an hour, hugging me, holding me, comforting me. Then, when there were no more tears, I said, "I'm gay." With those words I unlocked the cage and set myself free.

# Chapter Three

## Telling the Tale

I chose a true friend to make my first proclamation of my homosexuality. Although Jeff stared through dazed eyes, it was not because I had said I was gay. Rather, he was surprised that so many tears had been shed over something that to him was OK. "Who cares?" he asked. "You're my friend. I love you." With that, he turned to hug me. "It's a nonissue, Eric. An absolute nonissue." Then he asked, "Have you told your mother?"

I gasped for air. "Tell my mom? Are you crazy? I mustered all the courage I had just to tell you." My laugh reduced from a deep gasping to a nervous chuckle. "Tell my mother. Yeah, right."

"You've got to tell her. It's not like she's going to reject you."

I questioned his sanity

He didn't budge. "Come on, let's tell her."

"You're serious?"

"Yes."

Without another word, Jeff started the car and drove the 15 minutes to my mother's house.

"I can't believe I'm doing this," I said. "What the hell am I supposed to say? Hi, Mom. I'm a fag."

"Something like that. Do you want me to go in with you?"

"No, but thanks."

Jeff waited in the car as I walked up the driveway of the house I'd lived in for 18 years. I looked through the window of my old bedroom. The room held disturbing memories: Inside, I had experienced my first sexual urges for boys and had hid my folder of photos of attractive guys. The room had been a sanctuary that harbored my secret from the cruelty of the outside, and although I had been afraid, I was able to fantasize safely behind closed doors.

I had walked up this driveway thousands of times before. This time, however, I would walk in a "straight" man and come out a gay one.

"It's me, Mom," I called, as I opened the leaded glass door and made my way to the TV room where Mom spent most of her nights since Dad had died. My eyes were glazed with sorrow, and my nose was still stuffed up.

"Jesus, Eric, what's wrong?"

"Mom, I have to tell you something."

"Here, sit down," she said. "What's the matter?"

I sat on the old couch that wore the nostalgic smell of "Mom." I lowered my head, and my convulsions started again. Next came tears from a well I thought had dried up. I sat, shaking, sobbing, and put my hands to my face while Mom went for Kleenex. After wiping away the first round of tears, I realized there was no way out. I hadn't devised a back-up excuse for my tears. I would have to come clean.

"I'm gay."

"You're gay?"

I nodded.

Mom hugged me, "Oh, honey, that's OK. That's no big deal. Really, it isn't. You know I have lots of gay friends."

"You do?"

"Sure. Georgia and Nancy, and you remember Carol. And you know John sleeps in two camps? It's no big deal, sweetheart," she said as she handed me some tissue. "Hey, I'm a card-carrying member of PFLAG."

"PFLAG? What's that?"

"An organization that supports gays and lesbians. I've been a member for years."

"You have?"

"Sure, honey," she said. "I'm a gay rights supporter. In fact, next month I'm being honored by the Orange County Elections Committee, another gay organization."

"You are?"

"Yes. Last year my friend Cathy and I went. She said to me, 'Margaret, I've never seen so many gorgeous men in one place in my life.' Why don't you go with me this year?"

"OK, sure, Mom."

"Why don't you call your brother and tell him?"

Was I hearing this? Georgia, the bigwig lawyer I had known all my life, gay? John too? How come I didn't know this before? A gay organization is honoring my mother? Did she just say I should tell my brother?

My older brother had never supported gay people, or any other minority, for that matter. At 25 I still felt great anger toward him and his myopic views. The thought of telling him was met with a resounding, "No way in hell!" My initial fear, however, lasted only a few seconds before changing to an impulse for revenge. My tears subsided as a warlike preparedness took hold. I wouldn't be merely proud to tell him; I would shove it down his throat. For all the homophobic comments he had made, for all the racial slurs he had slung, for all the hatred he possessed, I would return the deed. I picked up the phone and dialed.

"George, I've got something to tell you."

"Yeah, what is it?"

said all fags should be shot?"

,d."

gay."
"ᴄ    s cool."

Somev...ere between the ages of 17 and 28 my brother had grown up.

Jeff, after waiting in the driveway for God only knows how long, drove me back to my condo and to my two homophobic roommates.

When my roommates were not home, I phoned my new gay friends. I talked freely yet quietly. When they were home, however, conversations were sterile, without an inkling of homosexuality. I lived in a closet with a revolving door. The elation I felt when I talked as an out gay man was addictive. So I began to tell select people my truth. I was delighted with the loving, supportive responses I received, and the absolution I felt inspired me to tell person after person. I grew addicted to speaking honestly. I even worked up the courage to tell my 87-year-old grandmother. "Well, as long as you're happy, Eric. That's all I care about," she said.

Each success inspired a new call, and soon I realized I would be calling everyone on my 72-person phone list. I drew two columns next to the names, labeling one *yes* and the other *no*. No longer willing to fear, not wanting to play the game of who knows and who doesn't, I decided to jump in headfirst and get it all over with. The people in the *yes* column were my true friends. Those in the *no* column were not.

There I sat, marker in hand, dialing number after number in alphabetical order from my telephone list. I began by crying for the first few numbers and then grew desensitized to the emotional process. I started with the 15-minute speech and soon shortened it to, "Hello, this is Gumby. Are you sitting down? I have something to tell you."

I now look back at the poor saps whose last names started with "A." They got the tears and oration. By the time I reached the W's, I was down to "Hey, Wes, it's Gumby. Just calling to let you know I'm gay." Soon I had told almost everyone but Coach Paul Wood.

During my time in high school, Paul had encouraged me to believe in myself and my running abilities. He nurtured me in all facets of life. Ten years later he was one of my closest friends and the man I respected most. Paul had promoted me within coaching circles and had helped push my career along by dropping my name when appropriate and by proofreading my manuscripts. He even resigned as head coach to become my assistant so that I could benefit from the title. He respected me as one of his own kin, having once written in a letter of recommendation, "If I were to choose qualities for my own children, I would choose them to be like Eric." Devoutly religious, Paul also served as deacon in the Baptist Church. He was old school in both philosophy and religion. Although he wasn't a right-winger or religious zealot, he shared most of the church's ideologies. I questioned how he would react, remembering the time he was hurt to find out that one of his sons had moved in with a girl without marrying her. If he was upset about that, what was he going to think of me? After all, he wished his own children could be like me. Although I feared losing him in my life, I owed him the truth.

An hour before track practice I said, "Paul, can we talk for a minute?"

"Of course. What's on your mind?"

I motioned for Paul to follow me to the cold, dilapidated room under the bleachers, closing the thick metal door to ensure our privacy. The lights were off, my face visible only through the slivers of light that seeped through the thin windows in the doors. We sat on a cold training table. "I'm going to tell you something..." Before I got any further, I broke into tears. Worried I might bawl for an hour, I changed my plan, opting to just blurt out the facts, "I'm gay."

With less than a moment's pause, Paul moved to embrace me. "Eric, now I'm going to tell *you* something. So is my eldest son." I cried as I had not cried since my father's death. Paul assured me that it made no difference to him. He still loved me. "And I always will," he said. I would not lose this father too.

"What repercussions might this have on my coaching?" I asked.

"I'm not sure," Paul said.

I recalled the Briggs initiative from when I was 10 years old and feared homosexuality might be justification to fire me. Such a notion might seem ridiculous now, especially for a guy whose mother is a judge. At that point, though, I had no idea what an open-and-shut civil rights violation that would have been, and I was ignorant about the case law that protected me. To further ruffle me, I feared that walk-on coaches who "serve at the pleasure of the principal" could easily be "not rehired." Paul had always told me that the principal "doesn't have to fire coaches; he simply doesn't rehire them the next year." Such nebulous phrases as "serve at the pleasure of the principal" and "not rehired" gave the principal furtive power. As I would later learn, my concern was legitimate.

"I love coaching," I told Paul. "My runners are my family. They mean everything to me. But I can't live this lie any longer."

"It's better to be honest and to deal with it than it is to walk in constant unrest," Paul said. With that in mind, I made my way to the main offices, bent on informing the administration.

I knocked on the door of Darrell Stillwagon, the the school's vice principal. Darrell had been at Huntington Beach for 29 years and was known affectionately as Mr. H.B. His children had attended school there, and he had served as a teacher, a coach, and our district's most respected school administrator. An athlete, Darrell was as thin as a distance runner and looked good for a man in his mid 50s. But he tended to overwork himself. He could be found in his office at 7:30 in the morning and at a basketball game at 9:30 that evening. His devotion to the school could be seen in every person he spoke to and everything he did.

Darrell was the balm for whatever ailed our school, and he handled chaos wisely. I recall him rushing to the scene of a fist fight on campus one afternoon. A hundred students circled around the teen gladiators, preventing security officials from stopping the fight. Instead of yelling at the students to disperse or pulling them aside one by one, he merely pointed his Polaroid and began snapping photos. The students immediately cleared out of his way.

Darrell invited me into his office. I closed the door behind me, signaling that what I needed to talk about was serious. "I need to tell you something," I said. "I just got through talking to Paul, and he recommended I tell you too." I paused. "I'm coming out."

"You're coming out as being gay?"

"Yes."

After my decree he stood up and walked over to me. Laying a hand on my shoulder, he asked, "Do you feel a weight has been lifted from your shoulders?"

"Yes. I finally feel I can breathe. I'm feel much lighter and happier."

Darrell conveyed, as he always did, a strong message of support. "You're not alone, Eric. There are many other gay teachers, both at this school and within the district. I even know a gay principal. But they're all closeted." He then spoke of how marvelous my generation was and how we were rapidly starting to accept gay issues, pointing to President Clinton's proposal of allowing gays in the military as an example.

"Can they fire me for this?" I asked.

"I don't think so. It's no big deal, Eric. Tell you what, let me go find Jim Staunton, and the three of us can discuss it."

Several years earlier, Darrell had applied for the position of principal, but to the surprise of most, the position was given to James Staunton. Staunton was short, around 5 foot 7, and had a serious administrator's face. He walked the campus in a suit and tie, with a walkie-talkie in hand, looking like a Secret Service agent. He had bounced around the district from one school to another, starting as a teacher and progressing through the ranks of the administration. He landed his first principal position at Huntington Beach. At the time I had no problems with him, although I occasionally found him short-tempered.

Staunton entered Darrell's small office wearing a power suit and holding his ubiquitous walkie-talkie. He sat beside Darrell and assured me all was fine. "Darrell filled me in on what's up," he began. "It's fine. You can do with the knowledge whatever you like. I don't recommend you make an announcement over the P.A., but you can do what you want." I was relieved at the assurance of continued employment. I thanked him, then talked a few minutes more, discussing the misery I had experienced, the pain and isolation of high school life, and how cathartic it felt to finally come out. I left the office confident, relieved, and validated.

I walked across campus to my runners, who had been waiting longer than usual for me to arrive at practice. As I walked, I reached into my pocket and pulled out a tattered sheet of lined paper, a resignation speech I had drafted the night before, fully anticipating this would be my final day as cross-country coach at Huntington. As I walked across our European-style campus, I joyfully ripped the speech into unrecognizable pieces and tossed them into a trash can.

I addressed my athletes, "Boys, I'm sorry I'm so late today. I've been in a meeting with the administration. I've had some hard times lately, but things seem to be working out. Some things are happening that should allow me to be a lot happier. I don't want to tell you what's going on just yet, but I assure you this coming season will be much more fun than last year."

Afterward, I worried about Ben. He had been competing at a higher level than the other runners had, preparing for the 9:10 two-mile he so desperately sought. He would be training heavily for a few weeks, with me as his constant companion. I knew he would want to know just what "things" were affecting my life, but I questioned the wisdom of telling him now, as he was focusing on qualifying for the state meet. Would it be better to tell him the truth and let him deal with it or not tell him and leave him to wonder? Over the next couple of days, I began to assess Ben's attitudes on the subject. Over this same time period I bought myself a ring and some new clothes. I changed my hairstyle and even got dress shoes to wear with my suit (instead of the running shoes I had worn to Ben's mom's wedding). Coming out of the closet boosted my self-esteem, and for the first time I felt good about buying things for myself.

Ben had to know something was up. His coach was wearing jewelry. He'd never seen that before. Nor had he seen me wear clothes that weren't left over from the '80s. On top of those changes, I had places to go that I couldn't tell him about.

He kept asking, "What's going on, Coach?"

"Nothing, Ben. I just decided to be happier."

A few days later, in a total coincidence, Ben told me about a party he had attended with his father. "There were all these gay guys there," he said. He made fun of it, referring to it as "weird." That made me uneasy.

I asked Ben if he was OK with it, and he replied, "Of course! I just thought it was funny—all these gay guys eating hot dogs." His facial expression suggested a sexual connotation. I decided Ben deserved the truth; I would tell him that day, right after practice.

After Ben finished his 16-by-400-meter workout, I joined him for a 20-minute cooldown jog. We were alone in the stadium. I had already determined that the track would be the best place to tell him. After all, it had served as our mutual home and the basis of our friendship. We finished the cooldown, and as Ben's heartbeat began to slow down, mine rose, pounding with the power of a seasoned distance runner.

"Ben, we've got to talk for a minute." We walked down the track's straight-away. "You know we're going to be spending a lot of time together the next few weeks," I said.

"I sure hope so," Ben replied.

"I think you should know what's going on with me."

"I think so too, Coach."

"I know I joke around with you a lot," I said. "But this time I'm not joking around." I looked into his eyes, "This is the hardest thing I've ever had to say to you, and I'm not sure how to tell you this, or even why, but I'm going to anyway."

Ben replied with a sarcastically inquisitive, "OK."

"Ben, I'm gay."

His eyes narrowed, and his head thrust forward. "No."

"Yes," I said as I nodded in affirmation.

Ben's head shook in short horizontal twitches, "N-a-a-ah."

Mine in vertical, "Ye-a-a-ah."

"No way! Really? No way, Coach. What about what's-her-name? And? Really?"

I said nothing.

"Serious, Coach?"

"Serious, Ben."

The realization sunk in.

"Hey, that's all right," he said. "Really."

The scene grew peaceful.

"I'm cool with it, Coach, really I am." He embraced me.

Ben and I were planning to have dinner with his mom that night. Jovial and warmhearted, Kathy Flamm was undoubtedly the one from whom Ben had inherited his charming sense of humor. I told Ben to go home first and tell his mom. I asked him to page me and tell me if she had a problem with it so that I would know if I should come for dinner.

A few hours later I received his page. My voice-mail message said, "Mom's cool with it. We're having another one of her vegetarian meals. Pretend you like it." When I arrived that night, Kathy opened the door. "I'm sorry we're having a vegetarian meal, Gumby, I know you like *meat*."

I couldn't help laughing. "So it doesn't bother you?" I asked.

"Gumby, you have done more for Ben than any other person in the world. How can I not love you?" Ben came out of his room. "Hey, my gay coach is here." He laughed, smiled, hugged me, then added, "Mom, we should be having hot dogs tonight."

For quite some time Ben would be my only runner to know. He would go on to run his 9:10 two-mile, socialize the Dynamic Duo into the team, then fly off to the University of Wisconsin.

*　　*　　*

A few months later, toward summer's end, Ben was in Wisconsin, and I was sitting in Dan's hot tub, skillfully dodging questions about why I didn't want a wife, even if she were a non-smoking, sport-psychology–loving, running goddess. I dodged, all without lying, the cover-piercing questions. But I knew the charade would have to end. If I were to coach my runners, they would eventually have to know me, the real me.

Week by week, my desire to tell the team grew. To do so, however, would take more courage than I possessed. I first needed to build up a bank of positive coming-out experiences with my former runners. Perhaps after telling them, I would find the courage to tell my current runners.

With that in mind, I began to confide in my alumni. Historically and currently, my graduates have evolved into friends of mine. They continue to hang around and display interest in how my current team is running. I, in turn, never give up the role of coach, continuing to look over their training regimes.

The choice of which alum to tell first was obvious: Matt Fulvio.

Matt was an eccentric and profound character, an intellectual, the product of a curious household. Television was outperformed nightly by National Public Radio, the *Oxford English Dictionary* was the most read publication in the house, and an exciting Saturday night involved witty conversation.

One of my greatest victories came when I defeated the entire Fulvio family at Scrabble. A competitive game of Scrabble, in the presence of formidable opponents, was the equivalent of a Fulvio family Gettysburg. The dining room table transformed into a battle zone strewn with several dictionaries. All words, in all languages, were acceptable.

Matt's intelligence and maturity enabled him to fit in with his father who has a master's degree, his mother who has two master's degrees, and his sister who scored 1,400 on the SAT when she was 12. Unfortunately, home was pretty much the only place he fit in.

Matt's liberal and educated upbringing also brought a sense of humor that few understood. I learned a lot from him. In fact, it was Matt who taught me what the rainbow flag and pink triangle symbolized. At age 17 Matt explained how Hitler used the pink triangle to identify the gay men he tortured and executed in Nazi Germany. Matt credited the gay community with taking back the sign, disempowering its once evil nature. He then reeled off facts about the history of the rainbow flag, Harvey Milk, and San Francisco. After that, I began chasing cars sporting the gay pride sticker to catch a glimpse of the driver. *Is he cute? Is he cute? Damn, a lesbian!*

Matt's liberal attitudes made him a solid bet for a positive response. Hell, he was even living in San Francisco. So I phoned.

"Matt, I have to tell you something."

"Gumby, you always tell me things."

"Yes, I know. But this time it's more serious." I skipped a beat and then said, "Matt, I'm gay."

"Really?"

"Yes. Today is my coming-out day."

"Congratulations, Gumby. Now you can be free."

My revelation didn't surprise Matt. Later, he would offer some of his characteristic wisdom to me: "You know, Gumby, I'll spend the rest of my life trying to prove that I'm straight. But you, you're free to be who you are without worrying about people having the wrong impression." A few days later the mail brought a small brown package from Matt. In it was a figurine, a "Peanuts" cartoon character with arms stretched wide and a caption that read, "I love you this much."

I proceeded to tell other alumni, some who had long since graduated from college and some who had just graduated from high school. No matter whom I told, announcing my sexuality spawned feelings of power and pride, even a sense of invulnerability. The thrill of standing in opposition to the norm, to be at one with your truth, is an affirming experience.

Coming out to increasing numbers of people also heightened my fear of certain other people finding out. When statements such as "Gumby, I think so and so knows" began to get back to me, the closet door suddenly slammed shut.

Part of me feared the team members would find out, and part of me hoped they would. I worried they might quit or that new runners might not join if they knew I was gay. But I also needed to tell them. Word would leak out anyway, and I'd be happier in the long run if I told them.

In time, I told most of my close alumni. Eventually, I felt it was time to tell the team.

* * *

Running long distances provides a coach an unique opportunity to carry on long conversations with his athletes. I had always wanted to know how my runners felt about homosexuality, so I learned to address the topic safely under the umbrella of other questions. I'd ask them, "How would you react if you found out your 15-year-old daughter was pregnant?" "What would you do if you found out your son had accidentally killed someone and nobody knew he did it?" "What would you do if your son told you he was gay?"

Such questions allowed me to gauge my athletes' views. Then, since the subject had come up, I was free to express my feelings. We ran the gamut on topics relating to homosexuality, including whether gay coaches should be allowed in schools. All along, I was testing the water while planting seeds of acceptance. We discussed biological perspectives, social theories, and ethical considerations. I didn't notice any attitudes against homosexuality on that year's team even before I came out, but this had not always been the case.

I remember having the same conversation with my team a few years earlier. I posed the same question: "What would you do if your son told you he was gay?"

"Kick him out of the house." "Get him laid." "Take him to a psychologist."

Once a young man answered, "I'd kill him."

Knowing I had shaped my athletes well, I decided to start by telling my team captain, Erich Phinizy. Remarkably dedicated, Erich had been one of my favorites since his freshman year. We had a rich history together, and I respected him for his dedication and maturity. Virtuous and in extremely good health, he had not missed a day of school since sixth grade. He was also the only runner who achieved the unparalleled record of never having missed a day's practice in four years. Erich's most ardent fan was his older brother, Harrison, who had graduated from Huntington three years earlier and now served as my assistant coach. Harrison did a fine job of coaching the younger runners and enjoyed it tremendously. I had told him about my sexuality several weeks earlier, and it came as no surprise to him. Harrison was a good friend and trusted confidant.

I decided to tell Erich first partly because he was team captain and partly because his brother already knew and was having a difficult time answering all of Erich's questions about me. Harrison and I opted to take Erich to lunch and then shopping at the running-shoe store, telling him somewhere along the way. I couldn't find the right time to tell him at lunch. Harrison kept steering the conversation in that direction, but I just couldn't do it. We drove to the store, and I tried on new shoes. Nothing about our conversation made it the right time to tell Erich, but I looked to the wall and saw a Nike "Just do it" poster. So I did. Somewhere between "Pass me the Nikes" and "size 11," I said, "Today is my coming-out day."

Flushed with confusion, Erich didn't know what to say. I understood his reaction; it was as if I had said I preferred bowling to running. But he was supportive. Later that day we discussed my life and experiences growing up gay. Erich accepted the knowledge and felt honored to know I trusted him with it.

After Erich, I told Joe Cucci and his parents, who were good friends of mine. Joe was a senior, and in our four years together I had become close to their family. His parents were products of the '60s and extremely liberal. So I told them before I talked to their son. They expressed their happiness for me in my newfound freedom. "Go ahead and tell Joe. He'll accept it," they said. They called Joe upstairs. "Joe, I just got through telling your parents something," I said, "and now I want to tell you. I'm gay."

"Really?"

"Yes."

"Oh, OK." He paused, "So what am I supposed to say?"

"You don't have to say anything, but are you OK with it?" I asked.

"Yeah, of course."

Brandon Yawata, who rarely spoke, was another senior on the team. I told him the next day after practice, and the news gave him no particular reason to speak now. I got nothing more than "Oh, OK."

I feared Jon Nichols, another senior, might not accept it as easily. I took him to lunch to tell him. As Jon began to unbuckle his seat belt and open the door, I said, "Hang on a second, there's something I want to tell you."

"Can't you tell me over lunch?"

"No."

"Well, make it quick, Coach. I'm hungry," Jon said, leaving the door slightly open.

"I'm only telling you this because I like you," I said. I've only told this to Erich, Joe, and Brandon." He looked at me with unconcerned eyes.

"Jon, I'm gay."

He looked at me. "That's cool, Coach. Can we eat now?"

I was stunned. Had he heard me?

"Jon, I'm not kidding."

"I know, Coach. It's cool. Can we eat now?"

I had told all of my seniors except Darin Johnson. Darin's mouth ran faster than his feet; telling him would have the same effect as my wearing a NOBODY KNOWS I'M GAY T-shirt to a school assembly. Besides, if Darin knew, the story would take on a whole new life. Darin lived in a different world and was good at telling stories.

Summer practice was going well, and in conversations with the four seniors who knew I was gay, we agreed there was no particular reason to tell others on the team just yet. They suggested I take my time and let the news trickle through the ranks. Even keeled, Joe said, "Let the freshmen get to know you first." It seemed like sound advice. So I decided the next phase would be to tell a few of the juniors.

I had confidence our relationships were rooted deeply enough to withstand the blast of my coming out. The juniors were, without exception, accepting.

I then told some of the sophomores. They too accepted the knowledge. Some temporarily refused to believe me, though, attributing it to another practical joke or research study. I had used my runners many times in my research projects, and they were used to my testing their attitudes. They were also used to my pranks. To them, I was the coach who cried "Wolf" one too many times. For those who did believe me, though, all went well. No one got upset, and no one quit the team.

With every runner I told, I secretly desired to hear one confide that he too was gay. I had to have at least one gay runner, if not two or three. Although I didn't think I had much of a chance of their confiding in me, since it had taken me 25 years to come out, I still hoped to hear it. It made me feel good to believe that at least one runner might take secret comfort in knowing he was not alone.

After outing myself to the athletes, I welcomed them to the club: the group of runners who knew about my sexual orientation. Being a member of the club had certain benefits. Foremost, it allowed them to laugh at the naive things nonclub members said. Darin was the primary target. He was the kind of guy who would sit on a bus and make ethnic jokes, not realizing a black kid was behind him. Not knowing I was gay, he freely made gay jokes around me and the other runners. In fact, one day we were warming up on the field of nearby Laguna Beach High School, where we went to run hills. Laguna Beach is a hilly gay mecca in Orange County, a world all its own. Darin said to me, "Hey, Coach, you like Laguna Beach, don't you?"

"Of course I do," I replied.

"You like all the gay guys in Laguna Beach, don't you, Coach?"

"Of course I do, Darin."

Darin thought he had just done a superior job of ripping me.

"Hey, Coach, what's the color of the carpet in the Boom Boom Room (a gay bar in Laguna Beach)?" He laughed at me, and the other runners laughed at him. He thought they were laughing with him. So he continued,

"Hey, Coach, do you find me sexy?" he asked as he came to my side and ran his hand up and down my chest while giving his best stereotypical gay act. This, of course, brought uproarious laughter from the rest of the team.

"Not really, Darin."

Through it all I maintained a straight face, without a trace of laughter. My runners, on the other hand, had come to a complete stop. Jon, Erich, Joe, Brandon, and the others were bent over from laughter. Darin, of course, thought he was Mr. Comedy and continued by trying to find out who I was attracted to.

"Do you like Joe, Coach? How about Erich? You like blonds, don't you?"

Through the cheers and jeers I stopped him.

"Darin, we need to talk."

I motioned him to come speak with me in private, while the rest of the team continued their laugh storm. Out of range of the team, I said, "Hey, they're not laughing because of what you're saying. They're laughing because you don't really know what you are saying." He looked at me with odd expression. "Darin, what they know and what you don't is that I *am* gay."

After conversing a minute or so longer, we returned to the team. The runners mocked, "Hey, Coach, you like Laguna Beach, don't you?"

"Hey, Darin, do you find Coach *sexy*?" Jon asked as he rubbed his hands on Darin's chest in the same provocative manner Darin had done to me.

We welcomed Darin to the club and asked him to keep it quiet, even though we doubted he would.

Unfortunately, covert clubs don't stay covert for long. Sooner or later someone is bound to figure out the secret handshake. Simon Bhavilai, for instance, found his way into the club by accident. Simon, the slow freshman who loved to run, was in the back of my van as we drove home from a workout. He grew tired and fell asleep, slumping out of view. I thought I had dropped all of the nonclub members off and began talking about the guy I was seeing. In my rearview mirror I saw Simon rise from the backseat. Not knowing what to say, he just sat there. I laughed, looked to the runner riding shotgun, and exclaimed, "Holy shit, I thought we were alone. Well, Simon, you learned something new today, didn't you?"

"Ah, yeah, Coach."

"Are you cool with it Simon?"

"Ah, yeah, Coach."

"Any questions about it?"

"Ah, no, Coach."

"Will you promise not to tell anyone?"

"Ah, sure, Coach."

I was pleased to have told much of the team without a single adverse reaction and was grateful the club members had kept my secret. But I still wasn't ready to come out to the freshmen, who were still getting to know me. I thought it best, with them, to wait until the beginning of school. My greatest fear was losing my most talented prospects, Dan and Tony. Part of me wanted to tell them so that the anxiety of not knowing whether they would stay on the team would end.

With school approaching, and in a momentary lapse of reason, I made a significant coming-out step. The team was having a movie night, and we drove to the store to buy candy. We then loaded up to head to the theater. I had already examined Dan and Tony for their sensitivity toward gay issues when the topic "accidentally" came up during our runs. Dan seemed all right with it, so I reasoned it might be OK to tell him. I was nervous, though, since I stood to lose so much with him.

"Dan, I'm going to tell you something I think you should know. It's something that most all of the seniors, juniors, and sophomores know. You will be the only freshman to know, besides Simon. I hope this doesn't upset you because I really want you to run for me. Dan, I'm gay."

"Really?"

I nodded.

"Hey, that's no big deal, Coach."

"It doesn't bother you?"

"Not at all. If that's who you are, that's who you are."

"Thanks, Dan. Do you think your parents will still let you run for me?"

"Well, hell, I'm not going to tell them!"

I didn't tell Tony that night because he wasn't with us. I would tell him the next day since I had agreed to take him to purchase new running shoes. Tony was not as verbal as Dan, so I didn't have as clear a picture of his views on homosexuality as I did with the others. I picked him up, and Erich and I drove him to our local running-shoe store. Once we were inside, a purposeful slip in speech came, something along the lines of "And if I weren't gay, it wouldn't matter." Tony looked at me with an odd expression, and I said, "Today is my coming-out day."

Tony's forehead vein bulged as he tried to decide what to say. But all he could say was, "Oh," and nothing more. I asked, "Do you know what that means, Tony?"

"I think so."

"It means I'm gay."

"That's cool," he squeaked.

At practice the next day Tony told me he had talked to his father and asked him what he thought of homosexuality. His dad didn't have much of a problem with it but had asked Tony, "Is there something you want to talk about?"

"Tony, your dad's going to think you're gay," I said. I told him he had better clarify things with his father. To do that, though, he would have to tell his father about me.

I had told my runners they could inform their parents if they wanted, but I secretly hoped they wouldn't. I saw no reason to open a can of worms. Ben's mom and Joe's parents knew, but I was close to them. I certainly didn't want the parents of a freshman knowing, especially the parents of a talented freshman. Now Tony had to tell his dad. He did, and Cheryl and Ricardo invited me over for dinner that night.

"Well, I guess Tony told you," I said.

Cheryl replied, "Yes, he did, Gumby. We want you to know we support you. Hell, we have gay friends at work."

An outgoing and entertaining woman, Cheryl was always good for a laugh and related well to the guys on the team because she looked 20 years younger than she was. Ricardo was more reserved but was one of the nicest guys I'd ever met. Together with Dan's parents, Liz and Stuart, they became the foundation of our fund-raising efforts. They helped organize six annual races for the team and wore their black HB cross-country baseball caps everywhere, even though Cheryl was the only one who looked good in it. Ricardo and Stuart hit it off as friends and even began running together.

Dan soon told his parents I was gay, and, like the Truebas, they supported me. They continued to invite me to their home, and Stuart continued to offer me beer. I felt lucky to have runners with such great parents.

In the final days before the new school year, I decided to come out to the rest of my team. I told them individually during a run or at the end of practice. Usually I told them nonchalantly. I might say something on a run like, "My boyfriend and I saw a great movie last night" or "Oh, my God, that guy is cute," as we ran past one of the hundreds of reasons I love Huntington Beach: the surfers. When surfers run across the Pacific Coast Highway wearing their tight black wetsuits, rolled down to their waistline, with a surfboard under one arm, they are the sexiest guys alive. The sheer eroticism of watching the sun dance off their muscular bodies and sun-bleached hair makes the beach path one of my favorite running routes.

I told the rest of my runners with the same degree of success I had told the others. I suspect they felt a fair amount of peer pressure to accept it. After all, what were they going to say surrounded by 15 teammates who accepted me? Peer pressure can be a positive thing, and in this case it was. We started the school year with 20 runners, all of them in on my secret.

# Chapter Four

## The Duo's Freshman Year

*Cross-country*

School began, and with it came a new set of fears. I wondered if my athletes would leak my secret into the rest of the student body, but I would not have to fear long. Although the runners had done a fine job of keeping the knowledge to themselves that summer, the challenge was not met successfully when school began. Word began to spread, slowly at first, then quickly. In hindsight, I realize how ridiculous it was to expect teenagers to keep such a secret.

Unprepared to deal with the entire school knowing, I called my runners into a prerun meeting. I intended my speech to be sort of a "State of the Union" address. "Rumor has started to spread throughout the school," I began. "I just want you guys to know that it might be in your best interest not to tell your classmates."

"Coach, I think it's a little late for that," Joe said.

"Why? How many people know?" I asked.

"Word spreads quick, Coach," Jon piped in.

They were correct, and a few weeks later the unthinkable occurred—in front of an entire class.

"OK, guys," I said, "Your teacher has left instructions for you to work on your photo journals and to turn them in at the end of the period. Any questions?"

A bold student raised her hand. "Yes, Mr. Anderson, is it true that you're gay?"

Immediately, embarrassment washed over me. I wondered how to respond, and a couple of possibilities came to me: "That's none of your business" and "Where did you hear that?"

Instead I answered, "Yes, I am, Kristen. Now are there any questions about the assignment?"

*Boom!* The proclamation traveled through school faster than the time it takes the guy behind you to honk after the light turns green. I left class an openly gay teacher. The next period students began to ask me about my sexual orientation in class.

Word spread to one of the seniors who had run cross-country for me the year prior. Schön Cooper was really a sprinter but joined cross-country because he loved the team's family atmosphere. Although he was not on the team now, he was one of my runners at heart. Schön was intelligent, liberal, and one of the funniest guys I had ever met. He could imitate anyone and did an especially good job of "acting gay." He phoned Harrison, my assistant coach, asking, "Is there something going on with Gumby?" Harrison told him to call me.

"Hi, Coach, this is Schön."

"Hey, what's up?"

"Not much. Just calling to see if you want to do lunch sometime soon. I want to talk to you."

"Sure, Schön. How about tomorrow?"

We sat at the table discussing everything except homosexuality. Schön came up with an amazing array of topics that were serious enough to warrant a meeting with me but none of which he could maintain long enough to convince me that they were legitimate problems. Finally, I said, "Schön, you brought me here to ask me something. So ask it."

"I've heard that you're gay," he stated.

"Yes, I am."

Schön began to shake. It was a familiar sight.

"I take it you're going to tell me something?"

"Well, I think I'm gay too, but I still like girls."

Soon Schön dropped his "bi" label and began the process of coming out. It was helpful for him to have me there. He knew he could confide in me and trust me. I looked out for him, watched over his dating, and kept a close eye on his activities. I cared a great deal for him and still do. Today he is one of my best friends.

As word of my sexuality continued to spread around campus, some students were brave enough to inquire about me in person. I answered their questions as honestly and professionally as I could. I also answered them with fear of administrative repercussion. The resident substitute job is appointed on a year-to-year basis. I'd had the job for two years, then taken a year off to finish my degree. I had reapplied for the job again this year and really wanted it.

The resident substitute acts as a daily substitute teacher on campus. The teacher shows up to school in the morning and receives a class assignment. The job came with a guaranteed paycheck and allowed me to teach and coach on the same campus. I hoped I would, someday, land a full-time position as a health teacher at Huntington Beach. For now, though, this was the best I could do.

I thought I had things stacked in my favor. Darrell had informed me that the resident substitute position was designed for a head coach who was not a full-time teacher on campus—exactly what I was. Besides, the staff constantly requested me as a substitute. The students liked me, and the teachers knew me.

I walked into Darrell's office a few days after applying for the position. "Any word yet?" I asked.

"I'm sorry, Eric, but you didn't get it."

"What? Why?"

"Principal's prerogative," Darrell said, looking away.

"Principal's prerogative? That's it? That's the reason?"

"That's all he's saying, Eric. That's all I can say."

"Who got the job?"

"A football coach."

I was furious. This, even though I had coached at Huntington Beach for seven years. I asked Darrell the football coach's name.

"Doug Brown," he replied.

"Doug who? I've never heard of him."

"He's new."

"Wait a minute. Is he a head coach?"

"No, an assistant."

"I thought the position was designed for a head coach."

"That's what we've always used it for."

This was the first time Darrell was short, almost callous, with me—quite unlike him. He was either acting as a puppet for Staunton and disagreed with what the principal was doing, but couldn't say so, or his attitude about me had changed since I had come out.

Losing the resident substitute position upset me, but I could survive financially. The position paid the same as regular substituting but was preferable since it guaranteed a job on Huntington's campus. Now I would have to regress to regular substituting, which meant I would be called each morning at 5 o'clock to be given a teaching assignment at one of the six high schools in our district. Each school had a different bell schedule, making it difficult for me to be at practice on time. My athletes would never know exactly when I would arrive at practice. Some days it was 1 o'clock, and other days it was 3, all because Staunton would not rehire me.

I began to worry about my career. I had dreamed of becoming a dynamic health teacher and distance-running coach at Huntington Beach, but if Staunton wouldn't hire me as a substitute, would I ever land a full-time position?

I knew worrying would only distract me from coaching, so I focused intently on my team. Tony and Dan ran their first several freshman races together and even tied for first place a few times. As the season progressed, Tony began running faster than Dan, so I put him on varsity. Dan ran, and won, all of his frosh/soph races. I brought a date to watch their first Orange County cross-country championship meet. I feared parents might somehow figure out my "friend" was more than that. "OK, you're just my friend," I told him. "If anyone asks, you're a runner, and we've known each other for years." He, in turn, told me to relax and tried to assure me that no one would suspect unless I stressed about it, which was precisely what I was doing. I introduced my date to Tony's mom, Cheryl, and when he wasn't looking, she flashed me two enthusiastic thumbs up. Pretending to worry that she might try to steal him from me, I turned to her and jokingly exclaimed, "No! You can't have him! He's my boyfriend!" while shooing her away. The race turned out to be great for the Duo; they finished as the third- and fifth-fastest freshmen in Orange County.

Near the end of the Duo's first cross-country season, word leaked out that a handful of brave students at nearby Fountain Valley High School had decided to do what no other group had done in Orange County. Don and Ron Katz, twin boys, began a quest for human dignity by forming the Gay-Straight Alliance on campus. Ron had come out to select friends at Fountain Valley. Don was suspected of being gay but denied it at the time. With the help of friends, they began meeting informally during lunch. They had been doing so for quite some time before anyone took notice. The group had actually formed the year before and found an advisor in Dr. Mike Poff, a friend of mine from my student teaching days at Fountain Valley. Dr. Poff was a large, gentle man, honored by students and respected by staff.

The group grew to 20, and with the larger numbers word of the club spread throughout the school. Homophobic parents and students soon began to complain. A member of the opposition, Bobby Dodge, a senior, formed what he called the Future Good Boys of America club. The club's sole purpose was to prevent the GSA from meeting. Irate students and parents took the matter to our school board's December meeting. (Fountain Valley was in our district, so we shared the same school board.)

The board meeting grew crowded and combative as both sides came to make their feelings known. Word had leaked to the press, who also showed. Speaking against the alliance were Dodge, members of his group, and individuals representing the religious right. In favor of the alliance were Dr. Poff, several of the club's members, and one teacher, Mike Hennigan, who stole the show.

Mike, my student teaching advisor at Fountain Valley, the football coach and athletic director in whose desk I had found the Bible and the man I'd pegged as a dumb jock, spoke in favor of the gay-straight alliance. I had grossly misjudged him. I had not expected him to side with us. Yet Mike stood up and delivered an emotional and shocking speech for all, including the press, to hear.

In his speech, for the first time publicly, Mike revealed that his own son Patrick, an alum of Fountain Valley, the student voted Best Overall, and an all-American offensive guard, was gay. Mike showed great courage revealing his son's sexual orientation to the public, and the following morning the *Los Angeles Times* ran a heart-warming article covering the board meeting and Mike's story. The article concluded by reporting that the school board had postponed the issue for another month, needing time to fully research the matter.

Before the next meeting, in a vile demonstration, the FGBA organized a protest outside Fountain Valley. On one side of the street an angry mob of loathsome students waved signs that read, FOUNTAIN VALLEY…NOT FAGGOT VALLEY. They clamored for cars to honk in support of their cause, while the other side of the street was lined with people holding signs proclaiming their support of the GSA, and one that read, THE RELIGIOUS RIGHT IS NEITHER. Police were called in to keep the peace, and dozens of reporters showed.

To show my support, I decided to attend a meeting of the Fountain Valley GSA. After all, I was the only openly gay teacher in our district, a sad statistic since 551 full-time teachers worked in that district. Today, since I am no longer teaching in the Huntington Beach Union High School District, there are no openly gay teachers. Mike Hennigan, though, is now president of the Orange County chapter of PFLAG. I wanted to attend a GSA meeting but wasn't sure I would be allowed since I wasn't a full-time Fountain Valley faculty member. I feared that if the administration discovered me at the meeting without permission, I might somehow jeopardize the students' right to meet. So I decided to wait until I was at Fountain Valley on official business.

"Good morning, Gumby" was a familiar phrase. I heard it from Ellen, the woman who made the 5 A.M. call for substitutes. I had received this wake-up call nearly every morning since losing my resident-substitute position at Huntington Beach.

"Morning, Ellen," I replied.

"I have a health class at Marina, one at Huntington, and one at Fountain Valley."

"I'll take Fountain Valley."

I spent the morning subbing for Mike Hennigan, as he had taken the day off to appear on a TV talk show to discuss the alliance. That afternoon I had lunch with Dr. Poff. He filled me in on the details of the political happenings, and I secretly attended that day's GSA meeting.

Wearing a black leather jacket, I sat in the rear of the room, feeling like an outcast. Several FGBA members tried to enter; the FGBA had grown in membership and had drawn up an "anti-alliance" mission statement. They argued that homosexuality was sodomy and that the school should not allow students to meet to discuss illegal activities. (Sodomy is illegal between minors.) The FGBA petitioned to form a beer-drinking club on campus, under their skewed logic that beer drinking is also an illegal activity for minors, and since there was a gay club, they wanted a beer club. "Maybe if they get drunk enough," Dr. Poff joked with me, "we'll find out which ones *really* want to belong to the GSA."

The FGBA undoubtedly wanted to attend the meeting to intimidate the GSA members by identifying those in attendance. Ron Katz had already been threatened with a baseball bat by an FGBA member in the school parking lot. Because of such incidents, we decided their acronym stood not for Future Good Boys of America, but Future Gay Bashers of America.

The FGBA protested Dr. Poff's not letting them into the room, but he handled the situation in a smooth and civilized manner. While FGBA members argued about whether they had the right to enter, he orchestrated a sly escape of the GSA members through a back door. The FGBA members couldn't see the maneuver because Dr. Poff's large frame blocked their view.

I was among the last to leave the rear door of the classroom, staying just long enough to witness one of the FGBA members charge the Poff-blocked door. He hit Dr. Poff at full speed and bounced off him like a child on a trampoline. We reconvened in a room with no windows and a locked door, where the meeting took place without further incident.

I met some of the members of the GSA, including Don and Ron Katz. They were not large boys. In fact, they looked as if they belonged on my cross-country team. I wondered how they had mustered the courage to start the club. Moreover, I was amazed at how these boys, at age 17, had the guts to do more than I had done at 25. They were two brave young men. Most of the other members were women, possibly because it is easier for straight women to support gay rights than it is for straight men. I wasn't sure how many of the students were gay. All I knew was that one, Ron, was out of the closet.

During the meeting students discussed the most pressing issue, their rights. They didn't know much about equal access laws or the formal processes it took to deny club status to a group. No one in Orange County had done anything like this. I told the GSA members I had recently come out as a gay coach at Huntington Beach, which made me immediately popular with them. We then discussed the upcoming school board meeting and strategies that might sway the board to approve the club. They discussed the recent media coverage and condemned a few teachers and the school's principal for not supporting them. Principal Gary Ernst had received no direction from the district and consequently took a neutral stance; at least he did nothing to thwart the group. Ernst was, however, primarily upset that Fountain Valley was fast developing the nickname of Faggot Valley.

After the GSA meeting, I began to correspond with Dr. Poff via the Internet. I learned a week later that the boy who had used Poff as a trampoline had filed assault charges against him. The FGBA member claimed Dr. Poff had thrown him across the hallway. Dr. Poff presented several student witnesses attesting to the opposite. Unfortunately, none of those witnesses were adults, and the administration said they could not make a decision based solely on their testimony. I asked Dr. Poff if I should report what I had witnessed, but he feared that if I did, my presence might jeopardize the club's ability to meet. In fact, the administration asked repeatedly who the mysterious man in the black leather jacket was. In the end, the alliance was allowed to continue meeting, but Dr. Poff was removed as their advisor.

## Off-season

Cross-country season ended. Dan won the freshman league title, and Tony helped the varsity team win a league championship. Although the season was over, the team continued to train.

The January board of education meeting rolled around, and with it the fate of the Fountain Valley GSA. Erich and I arrived a full hour early, and, to my surprise, we had to park several blocks away. So many people showed up for the meeting that the main room, which held 250 people, overflowed. The district had anticipated such crowds and equipped an auxiliary room with an audio system so that we could hear the proceedings. Erich and I found seats in the overflow room, which soon filled to capacity, necessitating use of yet another room.

While waiting for the meeting to begin, one of my former Fountain Valley students spotted me in the crowd. Joel was a large boy who had said little in class but seemed to enjoy my teaching. "Hi, Mr. Anderson!"

"Hey, Joel. It's great to see you. How are you?"

"Really good. I'm at Long Beach State and loving it. I just wanted to tell you that you were such an inspiration to me, Mr. Anderson. Your class was the best I ever took. I'll never forget that experiment when you lit a glass of Bacardi 151, burned yourself, and then dropped it on the floor."

"Yeah, I remember that," I said. "The class smelled like rum for a month!"

"So why are you here?"

"To see what happens with the alliance."

"It's sick. Gay people at Fountain Valley," he said.

"Joel, there have always been gay people at Fountain Valley."

"Yeah, but these people don't hide it. And it's not normal for a guy to like a guy."

"You're right," I said. "But just because it's not normal doesn't mean it's wrong."

"The Bible says it's wrong."

I figured Joel would have been on my side. I mean, he had me, "Mr. Liberal," as his teacher. He had heard my lectures about not judging, about diversity, love, and variety. I figured he had learned from me, but I sadly discovered he had not.

"It's just not right in the high school," he said.

"What about gay teachers, Joel? Should they be allowed to teach?"

"Heck, no," he responded.

"Joel, do you know that I'm gay?"

"What? No!" he said as his jaw dropped open. "But you were such a good teacher."

Joel continued to shake his head as he moved away from me and returned to his friends. His spirit to fight the alliance seemed to have drained with my proclamation. While Joel's friends cheered the antialliance speeches, he sat still, with a confused look on his face. The world was not as black and white as he had thought. I turned around a few minutes later to discover he had left the auditorium.

For more than three hours people debated the merits of the gay-straight alliance. Half the speakers supported the GSA, and half did not. The speakers against the alliance wielded religious arguments in support of their position, lashing out at gays for a slew of stereotypical reasons. The speakers in favor of the alliance spoke more rationally.

It was past midnight before the speeches concluded. With the same anticipation a courtroom feels awaiting a jury's verdict, the crowd hushed. The school board asked for a legal recommendation from their lawyer, who solved the issue with a single, emotionless statement: "If we prohibit the alliance to meet, we will be violating federal equal-access laws." With that, the board voted. Four ayes and one nay. The GSA was victorious.

The FGBA left in a visible tirade, one of them pounding on a desk exclaiming "That's bullshit!" as he exited. Meanwhile, GSA members gathered to hug and congratulate one another. I approached Don Katz. "You made history tonight," I said. "I'm proud of you." Erich and I talked with the GSA members a while, then headed to Denny's with them for a late-night celebration.

The jovial atmosphere reminded me of how our team feels after winning a major invitational. Although it was 1:30 in the morning, the group was alive with a spirit of triumph. Erich too felt inspired. He looked in awe as these teenagers, no older than he, stood up against an ominous threat. Erich had a hard time standing up for himself, and he admired these teens for making a difference. They stood to lose so much, yet they fought for a cause that only some of them were born into. One girl told Erich that her mother disapproved of her involvement in the group, yet the girl maintained her active support. Another guy told Erich that he wasn't gay, but everyone thought he was because he was part of the club.

"Does that bother you?" Erich asked.

"Not really. I know who I am. Why should I care what they think?"

"So," Erich asked, "how did you start the club?"

Most of the members were only 17 years old, and here I was at 25, still afraid of my own gay shadow. I returned to school the next day inspired to be even more openly gay than I was. My euphoria would not last long.

*     *     *

Weighing the pros and cons of publicly coming out, I envisioned many possible scenarios: I might be fired, harassed, discriminated against, perhaps even beaten up. I might lose some of my runners. Parents might complain to the administration. One thing I didn't expect, however, was that my athletes would also be victimized by homophobia.

Each day I checked my mail before practice. The runners knew that if they wanted to talk to me before practice, they could catch me at my mailbox and then walk to the track with me. One day, during winter training, one of the runners met me there.

"What's up, Colin?"

"Not much, Coach. I just wanted to talk to you about something."

"So talk."

"There's this guy in my class who's always bugging me, and I don't know how to make him stop."

"What does he do?"

"He calls me a fag all the time and tells people I'm gay. He says all the runners are gay because you are."

I told Colin I would talk to his teacher and that he would do something about it. Still, the situation disturbed me. I didn't want my athletes harassed because of who I was. I debated addressing the team about it, not sure if doing so would create more of an issue than need be. In the end, I decided to be proactive. During our next team meeting I said, "If anybody harasses you in any way, for any reason, if they say something to you, push you, anything else, let me know. I'll take care of it."

After the meeting Erich asked me what had happened.

"Somebody was calling Colin a fag in class."

"That's crap, Coach. Something needs to be done."

"Don't worry," I said. "I'll talk to his teacher."

Erich, however, decided enough was enough. He began a quest for freedom on campus. Erich, who talked regularly to Ron and Don Katz, decided to create the second gay-straight alliance in Orange County, the Huntington Beach GSA. He hoped he too could enact social change. Ron and Don supplied Erich with copies of their mission statement and told him how to go about establishing the club. Erich solicited the help of a teammate, senior Craig Reade. Together they made their mark in the history of gay rights.

Craig and Erich had been good friends since their freshman year. Craig ran for the team during his freshman, sophomore, and junior years but had decided not to run his senior year so that he could devote more time to the school's Model United Nations debate team. Craig had won the highest award, the Gavel, at many top Model United Nation conferences. These experiences equipped him to handle conflict well. Erich had no similar experience. He was timid and afraid of confrontation. Like Erich, Craig held strong liberal convictions.

Erich and Craig found an advisor in my former journalism teacher, Jeff Button. Mr. Button was of the same caliber as Dr. Poff, garnering the respect of nearly every student in school. He could also drum up the support of other teachers and would not allow himself to be harassed by an administrator. At the same time, he was a wonderful mediator.

Erich and Craig filled out the necessary paperwork to form the gay-straight alliance and turned it in to Darrell Stillwagon's office. There was no doubt about whether they would be able to form their organization; the district had already decided that gay-straight alliances could meet under federal equal-access laws. Originally, religious groups who wanted to use the school's facilities for meetings had fought for the equal-access laws, which now allowed for any group that did not promote illegal activities. The only requirement was that a teacher supervise the meetings. Erich's club was soon approved.

More than 25 people attended the first Huntington Beach Gay-Straight Alliance meeting. To Erich's knowledge, only two of the female students were openly gay. Erich wanted a guest speaker for the next meeting and turned in the appropriate paperwork.

Staunton sent a note to Erich in class, requesting to meet with him about the guest speaker.

"What do you think he wants, Coach?"

"I have no idea."

In the meeting Staunton explained to Erich that equal-access laws prohibited his club from having a guest speaker. But he also questioned Erich about his motives in forming the GSA. He spoke harshly, so Erich answered stubbornly.

"What is your motivation for starting this club?" he asked.

"I don't know," Erich answered.

"What do you intend to do in the club?"

"I don't know."

"Did anyone put you up to starting this club?"

"No."

"I don't want any problems here, Erich."

"OK."

Erich was new to being treated so rudely. I felt particularly sorry for him because Staunton can be rather intimidating. The principal's style leads one to believe that every question is either loaded or leading to something loaded. Because of this, you never know whether he is on a fishing expedition. Erich later told me that Staunton's tone, rude and intimidating, strongly suggested he did not want the GSA on his campus. This upset Erich, and for the first time he found the conviction needed to stand his ground.

I was proud of Erich. At no time did I talk to him about founding the GSA on our campus. In fact, I was shocked that he did it. I never expected him to blaze a trail. But Erich needed to stand behind something, to make a pitch against the norm, to open himself up to controversy. He used the alliance to make his stand. It was a self-created rite of passage.

Erich began the student alliance at Huntington Beach for several reasons, but his sexual orientation was not one of them. Erich is straight. The alliance copresident, Craig Reade, is also straight. Of course, no one actually believed that Erich was straight, especially when he refused to discuss his sexuality. He simply stated, "It doesn't matter if I'm gay or straight." To most, however, not claiming heterosexuality was equal to admitting to homosexuality. Therefore, most students believed him to be gay. They began to harass him based on their assumptions.

*Track*

By the time track season rolled around in March 1994, Erich's gay-straight alliance had made big news at the school and brought much more attention to our team. The cross-country team now had a gay coach and a presumed gay runner. This, of course, made it a gay team, didn't it? Sadly, I fielded legitimate questions from truly sensitive individuals who would ask, "Is it true the whole cross-country team is gay?" With all this attention Erich became a bigger target than a newly washed car under a dangling telephone wire. But worrying about Erich was only one of the many stresses I had that season.

My lagging ability to recruit new runners also concerned me. Before I came out I found it difficult enough to recruit students to the minor sport of distance running. The change in the perception of the team from being a really good team with a cool coach to that of a "fag team" with a "fag coach" really hurt. Unfortunately, in distance running, numbers are crucial for success. The more runners a coach has, the higher the likelihood of quality athletes running for the team. In essence, all a high school coach has to do to establish his team as a top-level distance program is to recruit a lot of runners. Show me a team with 100 runners on it, and I will show you a damn good team, even if the coach is Bozo the Clown.

To add to my anxiety, Coach Wood, the head track coach, hired a new sprint coach, Pastor Dan Newmire. Dan was already the girls' head cross-country coach, a position he had held for two years. He knew I was gay and didn't approve of it. Although he never said anything to me directly, he voiced his disapproval to the girls on his team and to their parents. Dan tried to turn the girls' parents against me. It didn't matter much because our teams were entirely separate, the only interaction occurring when we held dual meets in cross-country.

In cross-country the home team is responsible for marking the course and running the finish-line management system. Dan was not a runner himself and had never coached distance runners. Therefore, I did the majority of the work. Whenever something went wrong with his team, he blamed me.

For one meet I had marked a course with a solid line of white chalk. The course ran directly over an undetectable sinkhole in the grass, the kind in which a runner could easily break an ankle. To avoid potential injuries, I circled the sinkhole with chalk and drew an X through it, the accepted mark of a dangerous spot. Dan did not know what the mark meant and did not show his team the course. When his team arrived at the X, the girls turned left, off the course. Dan blamed me, convincing parents I had purposely mismarked the course. One parent believed Dan and grew so irate that he decided to assert his manliness by literally pushing me around. Taller and stronger, he cornered me and thumped his fingers into my chest, proclaiming I had set the girls' team up. Seconds before bloodshed, two saviors arrived, Ricardo Trueba and Stuart Gaston. Stuart stood between the girl's father and me. Facing the man, he looked into his eyes and said, "If you touch our coach again, you're going to have a problem with the three of us." After that, Stuart could do no wrong, even if he did drink beer and liked soccer.

So we had a boys' coach who was gay and a girls' coach who was a homophobic preacher. Paul, however, had now hired Dan onto the boys' track team, forcing me to coach and attend meetings with him. It might have worked out if I had just coached distance runners and he only coached sprinters. One event in track, however, serves as the twilight zone between the distances and the sprints: the 400 meters, one lap around the track that is short enough to attract sprinters yet long enough to lure distance runners. Four hundred–meter runners usually run cross-country during fall, then train with both the distance runners and sprinters during track. In other words, Dan and I would be coaching some of the same athletes. I was infuriated that Paul had hired him since he knew we didn't get along. When I asked about it, Paul replied, "He's a good sprint coach and a good Christian."

In addition to worrying about Erich, stressing about my recruiting capabilities, coaching with a homophobe, and dealing with how the rest of the track team would treat the distance runners, I also worried about Tony. Between cross-country and track, he had taken several weeks off from training because of a serious laceration.

One day as we set out for our run, I looked back to find him just standing there. From a distance I yelled to him, "What's wrong?" I could swear he said, "My foot hurts," so I replied, "Walk back to the van and get some new shoes." I returned from the two-hour run to find a note on my car from Harrison: "Gums, had to take Tony to the hospital." I couldn't imagine what had happened, so I paged Harrison. Tony had attempted to hurdle a fence. He caught his leg on a rusty nail and suffered a deep and long laceration. When I had seen him standing there and asked what was wrong, his reply was actually, "I cut my leg." Imagine the dismay he must have felt when his coach did nothing to aid him, told him to get new shoes, and then set off on a run.

Although I worried about Tony's missing so much practice, the Dynamic Duo and I set new goals for the track season. We decided they would focus on the two-mile and aim to break the freshman school record of 10:10.

The first day of track came. Dan Newmire would be the sprint coach, and several of my cross-country runners would have to train under him. We actually gained a few new distance runners on the team, although it was fewer than usual. I began our first day of practice by delivering my standard "Welcome, we need you, we are fun, we are good, there are no cuts, but this is a hard sport" speech. Only this time I added to the end of it, "And by the way, I'm gay, and if you have a problem with that, this might not be the right team for you."

Our team ran the first race of the season against Edison High School. The Duo ran impressive times for freshmen. Dan ran a 10:38, and Tony ran a 10:45 two-mile. Fortunately, they didn't know how amazingly fast that was. If they had, what happened the following Thursday in a dual meet against Santa Ana might not have occurred.

It was one of those races that combined the perfect elements: great competition, a perfectly paced race, cool, still air, and two young runners purely talented and uninhibited by psychological limits. Ignorant bliss.

At the start of the two-mile race, the Duo placed themselves behind five elite Santa Ana runners. They didn't know they were racing key members of the second-fastest cross-country team in the state, and I decided not to tell them, seeing no reason to instill fear in them. I figured I'd sit back and see how good they were. Their pacing was perfect. They came through in 1:15, 2:30, 3:45, and hit the mile mark in 5:00. Their current personal records for the mile were 4:48 and 4:52, so they were only seconds slower than that for the first of two miles. Their desire to beat each other kept them going, and they finished the fifth lap in 6:16, on pace to break the school record, in only the second race of the season. I yelled, "Go for the record! Go for the record!"

They were shocked that they were on pace to break the freshman two-mile record. Just a week earlier we had set that as their seasonal goal. Today was only the second of 13 races in the season. At this point, they no longer cared about following Santa Ana's runners. They took to the lead. They pushed the pace, trading positions with each other. They finished the sixth lap in 7:37, and I quickly calculated that a 2:33 half-mile would push them to the freshman school record. They finished lap seven in 8:54 with just a lap to go, and I knew they were about to break the record.

I yelled until my voice grew hoarse. I jogged alongside them as they ran neck and neck the final 100 meters. "Arms! Arms! School record! Go for the record!" I glanced at my watch as they crossed the finish line, tied, in 10:07. Unbelievable! They had broken the freshman school record that had stood for over 20 years.

Things were going well for the Duo but not as well for Erich. The antigay slurs cast his way numbered several dozen a day. Erich typically handled these attacks by remaining silent. Continued bouts of taunting, however, began to erode his patience, and slowly he fashioned new strategies to deal with it. His most effective technique was to carry a microrecorder in his pocket. When someone began to harass him, he brandished the recorder and pointed it in that person's direction. The effect was astounding. Erich also learned that when he expected badgering from a group or individual within a group, he was better off walking directly toward that group, as opposed to avoiding the people. Walking into the lion's den has a surprisingly positive effect. Berating someone is far easier from a distance than up close.

Erich's persecution enraged me. I wanted to lash out at those who messed with him but knew I could not. Under my anger also lay a great deal of pain. I knew Erich had begun the alliance for himself and for the sake of closeted students, not for openly gay coaches. I also knew this was the best thing Erich could do for himself. Still, my heart was torn with guilt. If I had not come out of the closet, none of this would have happened, I told myself. Then Erich could have learned to stand up for himself by spending time with a psychologist, rather than leading the life of Job.

My guilt grew worse the day we left practice and found the word FAG scratched across the hood of his car. "Oh, my God," I said. "I'm so sorry, Erich. I'm so sorry." I could do little for him, except assist in the futile attempt to polish it out with rubbing compound. The damage alone was upsetting, but it took on extra significance for Erich: He had not yet told his parents about the club he had formed.

Darrell Stillwagon tried to help by issuing Erich a permit to park in the staff lot, but I knew doing so was no guarantee of safety. Vandals had attacked my car repeatedly in the same lot. I'd emerge from practice often to find that my brand new minivan had been keyed, spat upon, or had dents kicked into it. For weeks on end someone let the air out of the tires, and once someone gouged two deep trenches up and down both sides of the van, causing more than $2,000 in damage.

Worst of all, Erich returned home from school one day to find a message on his answering machine: "You're gonna die, you fucking faggot!"

Erich phoned me. "Coach, I got a death threat on my answering machine," his voiced cracked.

"You what?"

"Here, listen." He played the tape.

The message was scary. Not a hint of joking in it.

"I'll be right over."

I picked him up, and we drove to the Huntington Beach Police Department to play the tape for them. The officer on duty said he could do nothing about it, suggesting we call the phone company and talk to them. Erich was visibly shaken by the threat. On the way home he said, "That's it. I'm done with it. I'm quitting."

"You can't back down now," I said. "The damage is done. Everybody thinks you're gay already, and they think the whole damn team is too. If you back down now, you'll show them you can be pushed around, that we're not worth fighting for. You'll have failed yourself. I didn't encourage you to start this, but now that you have, for God's sake carry it through. Besides, what difference would backing down make now? It's too late."

I returned to school the next day with a microrecorder and Erich's tape. I approached each of the administrators, asking if they recognized the student's voice. None did. Meanwhile, Erich pondered the situation for several days before he decided to continue with the alliance.

The verbal harassment, telephone death threats, and vandalism to our cars made me realize physical violence could ensue. Such fear led me to teach my athletes precautionary measures. I instructed them to always enter the locker room in large numbers, never alone. They were told to leave practice in a pack, enter one car, and drive from car to car dropping off the others. I made my presence known in the locker room as best I could and always walked my athletes to their cars. Still, we encountered problems.

I was describing a workout to my athletes when a tardy runner scurried up the track to inform me about a problem in the locker room. I ran down the track, across the parking lot, and careened down a flight of steps to the locker room. I heard the loud and distinct voice of Jon Nichols, one of my runners. Before making my presence known, I slipped behind some lockers and listened to the following dialogue:

"Now say you're sorry," Jon said.

"I'm sorry."

"And say you're never going to call him a fag again."

"I will never call him a fag again."

"And say you're never going to shut his locker again."

"I will never shut his locker again."

Jon, I knew, could handle himself physically; he had a black belt in karate. I remained undetected behind the lockers and took silent pride in how he had handled the situation. I never saw who or how large the antagonist was. Whoever he was, he obviously regretted mistreating one of Jon's teammates.

On another occasion, while my runners were driving through the school parking lot, a carload of homophobes pulled alongside them, flipped them off, and yelled "Fags!" as they steered in front of them, blocking their exit. My athletes displayed maturity in choosing not to return any comments or foul gestures. They simply sat in the car and waited for the tirade to end. One of the runners took down the license plate number, and with that, I found the name of the student who drove the car. I filed a report with the administration, but nothing happened.

Amid these growing tensions, I again addressed the team. "The first rule is that you are never to engage another student in a physical confrontation," I began. "Don't think you're protecting me by pushing someone or starting a fight. You're not. Second, I want you to report any incident to me so I can help to handle it properly. Finally, if anything happens to you while you're driving or running and you're anywhere near the police station, make a beeline there." Discussions of harassment became commonplace at team meetings, and it hurt to see my athletes dragged into the den of discrimination for no act of their own.

I began to fear for Erich's and my safety. Erich was the most visible target and, unlike me, possessed no protective cloak of coach or teacher to hide behind. Nor did he possess my deep voice that could scare off almost any tyrant. Erich was soft-spoken and ill-experienced in dealing with strife. I decided it was time for us to gain some education in the art of self-defense. For expert instruction, I had to look no further than Jon Nichols.

I discussed the idea with Erich, but he was a pacifist and wanted nothing to do with fighting. I didn't like the idea of physical violence either, but I wanted to protect my straight teeth and unbroken nose. So I started taking lessons from Jon on the mats of our school's wrestling room. Together we practiced several days in a row, or, shall I say, Jon practiced on me for several days in a row. I learned slowly, but the beatings were sufficient motivation to learn faster. I learned a lot from Jon, especially that I was a lousy fighter. I left the sessions bruised and battered.

While I was volunteering as a human piñata one day, four football players entered the wrestling room to see what all the "heyaying" was about. Knowing the power of rumors, I took the opportunity to make the most of it. I quietly asked Jon to let me win the spar, and he obliged. For the first time in a week, I scored a few good moves and appeared to have decidedly won the match.

Sure enough, while subbing a few days later, a student asked, "Hey, Mr. Anderson, is it true that you're a black belt?"

"I have two black belts," I said, without lying. I used them to hold up my pants, but no one needed to know that.

From there the rumors grew. "Hey, Mr. Anderson, I heard you beat the crap out of some football player for calling you a fag in the locker room."

"Well, it wasn't exactly like that."

If you can make the rumor mill work for you instead of against you, you might as well do so.

While I took to the mats for self-protection, Erich took to the radio for promotion on KUCI. No major station, you could urinate farther than its radio waves traveled. Erich spoke about the origins of the alliance and where he wanted to take it. The show likely drew less than a dozen listeners, and its only caller was my mother. The program, however, did attract reporters from the *Orange County Register* and the *Los Angeles Times*. The next morning, photographs of Erich appeared on the front page of the Metro section of both papers. Unfortunately, Erich had not yet told his parents about the GSA.

Erich's mom took the news well. His dad did not. It made no difference, though, as Erich was bent on proceeding with the alliance. His dad, I am happy to say, eventually came around and is now proud of Erich's activism.

Soon after the newspaper coverage, CNN showed up asking to speak to Erich. Staunton refused to let the reporters on campus. This was standard procedure whenever there was news that could make the school look bad. Nonetheless, the mere presence of the media in front of the school created a buzz among the students. The gay-straight alliance was discussed in classes, at lunch, and in the school newspaper. Irate parents called the administration to voice their disapproval of the club, and Staunton asked me to speak with Erich to calm things down. He hoped to use me to influence Erich.

"They are meeting. Isn't that what they want? Do they have to make an issue out of it?" Staunton asked.

"I'll talk with him, Jim," I said.

I encouraged Erich to follow his beliefs.

In the midst of all this controversy, the greatest challenge was to coach as I always had, trying not to let the political whirlwinds affect the team. But you can't always separate your struggles from your passions. Who you are is part of what you do. I am gay, we did have an alliance, and it did affect the team.

As Erich battled homophobes off the track, the Duo battled runners on it. They were becoming the caliber of runners I had hoped for, the backbone of what I called the frosh/soph Dream Team. They set meet records in almost every relay race they entered. Things were running smoothly, right up until Dan Newmire struck.

One of the 400-meter runners failed to anchor a race for us. In the presence of Dan Newmire, the athlete said he would do it. Dan even thought it would be a good idea. But on the day of the race, he didn't show. We could have won the race had we had a fourth runner. I phoned the runner that night to find out why he had failed to show. After hearing his response, I wrote the following letter to Principal Staunton:

*Principal Staunton,*

*On Friday, March 25, I approached some of the male sprinters to find two athletes who desired to participate in a relay race the next day. I approached Dan Newmire and asked him if he would mind if I took a few of his runners to the meet. He gave me permission and suggested a few kids to talk to. I approached these runners and found two who desired to go to the race, one of whom was junior Pat Campbell.*

*The next day, Pat showed. The other runner did not. He told me Coach Newmire had been making fun of him for planning to attend. He said that it was no big deal, though. The following Monday, Pat told me that after I had left on Friday, Coach Newmire began ripping Pat and making gay jokes. One such remark was, "Are you going to get it up the butt by the distance runners?"*

I called for immediate action. None was taken. "Dan denies having said anything," said Darrell Stillwagon. The situation repeated itself a month later. I wrote:

*Principal Staunton,*

*On Saturday, 4/24/94, I was talking to junior Drew Neufeld about running cross-country next fall. He said he would like to and probably would. I told him that his sprint coach, Dan Newmire, had also said he would like him to run. At this point Drew said, "That's what he told you? He asked me why I wanted to be on a fag team."*

*I asked Drew to elaborate. Drew told me that on many occasions Coach Newmire has made derogatory comments*

*about the distance runners being a "fag team." Drew made*
*it clear that Newmire has done this several times. He*
*informed me that Newmire has told the team I am*
*immoral because God didn't create men to sleep with men.*

Nothing was done. Absolutely nothing.

I struggled with the lack of justice, amazed at how vitriolic
someone who claimed to be a Christian could be. The concepts of
love, acceptance, and letting God do the judging were alien to
him. I was despondent. I begged Paul to remove Newmire from
the staff. He defended the man, saying, "Coming from those guys,
I don't know how much is true." He told me he would talk with
Newmire "Christian to Christian." This brought to mind the
words of my literary hero, Oscar Wilde:

> *I have never come across anyone in whom the moral*
> *sense was dominant who was not heartless, cruel, vindic-*
> *tive, log-stupid, and entirely lacking in the smallest sense of*
> *humanity. Moral people, as they are termed, are simple*
> *beasts. I would sooner have fifty unnatural vices than one*
> *unnatural virtue. The real enemy of modern life, of every-*
> *thing that makes life lovely and joyous and colored for us, is*
> *Puritanism, and the Puritan spirit.*
>
> *Modern morality consists in accepting the standards of*
> *one's age. I consider that for any man of culture to accept the*
> *standards of his age is the grossest immorality.*

My frustration with Staunton was compounded by the attitude of
another individual, one of our own brood, a distance runner named
Martin Gallas. Martin, a sophomore, was a fine distance runner and
a valued member of the frosh/soph Dream Team. But Martin was
concerned about one person: himself. I had asked Martin to help Tony

earn his varsity letter by pacing him in a race against an inferior team and then allowing Tony to win the race at the end, earning him the required points toward his varsity letter. Martin had already earned his letter, so he agreed to help his teammate. With 100 meters to go, however, Martin out-kicked and beat Tony to the line. I was outraged and questioned why he was not willing to help his teammate.

Martin's parents brought the issue to the principal. They were upset that I would not ask Martin to do his best in each and every race. They didn't like my teaching their son that helping other athletes was unselfish. The principal questioned me after talking to Martin's parents.

I told him that track was a sport, and, as in other sports, we attempt to help our fellow teammates. This, I argued, developed sportsmanship and taught athletes to cooperate as a unit to accomplish a common goal. I even gained the support of the athletic director, who told the principal, "This is a common practice in track." Paul Wood also supported me. "I've been doing that for 28 years," he said. Ultimately the principal took the side of the parents and requested that I clear any similar situation with him in advance.

At this point Jim Staunton would support almost any claim brought against me, no matter how ridiculous. He would do nothing about Dan Newmire's oppressive behavior nor would he hire me as the resident substitute on campus. Now he would not trust my judgment as an experienced track coach. I feared he might try to get rid of me as the boys' distance coach. He could either fire me or not rehire me. If he were to "not rehire me," he needed a better person to replace me, and that was not likely. If he were to fire me, he needed a solid reason. He began looking.

In my heart I knew my dream of teaching health at Huntington Beach would not come to be, though I was in denial. I would have to find a different dream to pursue. Even worse, the team was harassed constantly now, especially by the football team, and the administration did nothing to stop it.

Despite these problems, the first competitive year ended successfully for the Duo. Both Dan and Tony broke ten minutes for the two-mile in track, far exceeding the 10:10 goals we'd set at the beginning of the season. They also both broke the freshman school record for the mile. They won several freshman championship races and gave me the hope I needed to keep coaching at Huntington Beach. It was a year that brought two runners to a level of competition neither they nor I expected. Their success gave me hope for our future, and it couldn't have come at a better time.

After the glory of the 1993 Dream Team and the fame of Ben Flamm's winning big meets, I was in a lull. The depression of a shrinking team roster, increased hostilities on campus, lack of administrative support, and the hiring of Dan Newmire made me question why I stayed at Huntington Beach. But these two fine harriers, Dan and Tony, were a gift. Three more years of coaching the Duo was something to stick around for.

For them the timing was perfect too. A coach's best years occur when he is struggling to make it to the top. The Duo came along as I was nearing the top. I had spent years learning, building my experience, developing my training program. I had established myself as a quality coach, published a book, and graduated with a master's degree in sport psychology. I was ready for the job. The Duo needed me to build their futures, and I needed them to salvage mine.

The end of the school year came shortly after the end of track season. Erich, Craig, Jon, Joe, Darin, and Craig graduated, Martin Gallas quit the team, and Erich accepted my offer to come back to join the coaching staff with Harrison and me. Giving him an assistant coach job was the least I could do; Erich's actions were worthy of a Purple Heart. He was a true hero. How do you thank someone for blazing a trail you were too afraid to blaze yourself? Sometimes just saying "Thank you" is not enough.

Coach Eric Anderson (left) runs along the train tracks with senior Erich Phinizy, who created a gay-straight alliance at Huntington Beach High School.

Coach Paul Wood (right) instructs Tony Trueba during the runner's freshman year.

From left: Tony Trueba after placing second in the county among freshmen, Coach Anderson, and Dan Gaston, who placed fifth. Two years later Tony became the fastest runner in the county, with Dan right behind.

Tony Trueba and Dan Gaston, the Dynamic Duo, relax after running in their section finals during their sophomore year.

Dan Gaston runs his way to a new school record and a meet victory in the 3,000-meter race.

Dan Gaston's father, Stuart, congratulates his son after he wins the Cal Poly S.L.O. Invitational.

Simon Bhavilai, the team's solid fifth man, stretches before the section finals during his senior year.

Tony Trueba finishes the final 200 meters of the 1996 California state meet.

Clockwise, from left: J.C. Strutzel, Jerryme Negrete, Jay Rivero, Jess Strutzel, Ricardo Trueba, Dan Gaston, Jacob Childs, and Tony Trueba gather in front of Independence Hall during their trip to Philadelphia for the Penn Relays.

Tony Trueba (center) and his parents, Ricardo and Cheryl, pose after Tony's final high school race, the 1996 California state meet, in which the team placed sixth.

Simon Bhavilai (left) and Tony Trueba relax before running a 4-by-1-mile race during their senior year in track.

Jennifer Spahr wins the Woodbridge Invitational during her junior year.

The team poses after winning the 1995 Orange County championship. Back row, from left: Harrison Phinizy, Jess Strutzel, Tony Trueba, Dan Gaston, Jerryme Negrete, and Erich Phinizy. Middle: Jay Rivero, Jacob Childs, Coach Anderson, Simon Bhavilai, Anthony Nguyen. Front: Jennifer Spahr.

Clockwise: Jess Strutzel (the county's fastest senior), Coach Anderson, Tony Trueba (the county's fastest junior and reigning champion), and Jennifer Spahr (the county's fastest junior girl) after winning the 1995 Orange County championship.

Jerryme Negrete runs with Jay Rivero and Jacob Childs at the 1995 Cal Poly Invitational.

Jacob Childs helps Huntington Beach win the 1995 Central Park Invitational.

Jess Strutzel, who quickly became one of the fastest 800-meter runners in the nation, helps his team win the prestigious 1995 Stanford Invitational.

From left: Luke Shelton, Simon Bhavilai, Ronnie Alvarez, Dan Gaston, Harpreet Mavi, Jacob Childs, Tony Trueba, and Coach Anderson (front) celebrate after the last track meet of Anderson's career at Huntington Beach.

# Chapter Five

## The Duo's Sophomore Year

*Cross-country*

We began the Dynamic Duo's sophomore year, my second year as an openly gay coach, at the Las Vegas Invitational. These yearly treks through the desert had been helter-skelter for the team since each had held unique misfortune. One year, dazed and confused by the radiant lights of Las Vegas, I backed out of a casino parking lot to hear a curious thud from the rear of my van. "You hit someone!" yelled a frantic voice. I stopped the van and discovered I had bumped into a middle-aged drunken pedestrian. His inebriation, however, likely served him well, as he was unharmed. The next year my van broke down in the middle of the Nevada desert, 35 miles outside Las Vegas. Tony's father, Ricardo, had to make three trips to and from the broken van to shepherd my runners into town. Other years had brought unfortunate incidents as well: a broken arm, runners caught in compromising positions with girls, and food poisoning.

This year the trip to Las Vegas was a pleasant anomaly. Nothing tragic occurred, except for our accidentally leaving a runner in the hotel room the morning of the race. He was in the bathroom when we left, and nobody heard his cries of "Wait for me!" He emerged from a taxi only moments before the gun sounded.

This trip was different in another way too: I was now an openly gay coach. District policy required that one adult supervise each hotel room. There were four hotel rooms and four male adults, including me. The rule was never enforced. All the coaches knew they had only state that they had each room supervised; no one would actually check on the coaches. Years prior, when I did not have enough adults to supervise the rooms, I placed a piece of Scotch tape across each door seal and told the athletes that if they left, the seal would break. There was no way to reconnect the tape from inside the hotel room. This year, however, I felt it necessary to adhere to the rules. I thought Staunton was on the lookout for violations so that he'd have a reason to fire me. The scenario raised many questions, the most fundamental being, *Should I stay in one of the rooms?*

I was in a catch-22. If I did not supervise a room, I could be held responsible for leaving my athletes unsupervised. On the other hand, if I stayed in one of the rooms, I could open myself to criticism from parents or athletes. I had submitted an overnight trip request to the district office that stated that Stuart, Ricardo, Harrison, and I would supervise the four rooms. The district looked over the form and returned it to me stamped with approval. So I decided to do as I had always done.

Sleeping in the same bed as an athlete was never a pleasure cruise for me, especially when I was closeted. As a closeted coach, I had slept in the same room, and even the same bed, on dozens of overnight trips with my runners. It was normal, never an issue—well, at least for them. For me it caused anguish for the obvious reasons: You're lying in the same bed as an athlete who, as most athletes do, possesses a well-defined and sexually attractive body. That, of course, is what everyone thinks of right off the bat. I frequently field questions on the Internet from gay men about my being an openly gay coach. They invariably want to know, "Do you look at them in the locker room?" "Do you ever get it on with your athletes?" "Do you find your athletes attractive?" In fact, I'm sure some people will buy this book because so many gay men have locker-room fantasies. The fact that I am a real coach, with real athletes, allows readers to merge their fantasies with my reality.

Fantasies are a wonderful thing, and, of course, I found some of the runners attractive. But fantasy is separate from reality, and this book isn't a true-to-life *Front Runner* love story.

As an 18-year-old coach who shared the same bed with 17-year-old athletes, I had strong sexual desires for those athletes. But that was the easy half of the torture. The other half came from my deep and abiding fear of being discovered as gay. I worried I would talk in my sleep, perhaps let out an "Oh, Bob." Such fear drove me to try to stay awake all night. If I didn't fall asleep, I couldn't talk in my sleep. This wasn't that bad on a one-night trip, but it took its toll during weeklong training camps. I tried to get my sleep in the late morning after the athletes awoke, but I suffered from migraine headaches because of the lack of rest.

The older I grew, the less desire I felt to sleep with the boy next to me. I began to view the boys more and more as my "kids." This made my sleeping arrangements easier each year I coached. Until I came out.

This year I also had to determine with whom I would share a room and whose bed to share. My fears of parental concern compounded the situation. In the past I had designated room assignments based on psychological design, such as who liked whom and who would (or would not) be rambunctious with whom. I abandoned that model this year, replacing it with room assignments based on whose parents I thought least likely to protest. I most often shared beds with the seniors, and we always slept four to a room.

At no time did I discuss the situation with the athletes. I assumed some students might feel uncomfortable sleeping in the same bed as an openly gay coach. But I didn't want to bring the subject up with them for fear their response might make things more difficult. I varied the rooms I shared on our many overnight trips so as not to make it appear I had a first choice, which I worried might lead to speculation. That way no one runner could be razzed for sharing a bed with me, because they all would have to at some time. Furthermore, in the unlikely event that a runner might accuse me of having tried something sexual, I would have other runners to support the fact that I did not try anything with them.

To further ease the situation, I slept in blue jeans. Climbing into bed wearing jeans served as a signal that sex wasn't on my mind. Ironically, I was often thought the one most ideal to sleep with because, "He doesn't snore or roll around." Of course I wasn't sleeping or rolling around. I was wide awake wearing blue jeans!

The Las Vegas Invitational went well, and we beat the other 13 teams for first place. Tony and Dan had improved tremendously over the summer. They both ran varsity and were our two top runners. In fact, Tony won the meet, his first-ever varsity invitational victory. Rarely does a sophomore beat all the juniors and seniors in a race with hundreds of runners. Cheryl was so proud of him that she began to cry after the race, saying, "That's my boy." Dan finished fifth, an amazing accomplishment.

While the Duo's moms, Cheryl and Liz, watched the races and took snapshots, their dads, Ricardo and Stuart, circled the course with their camcorders, shooting every minute of the race they could. They never knew where to run to film from next. Stuart called in his English accent, "Wait for me, Coach," as he struggled to keep pace with me. I could always tell when the Duo's parents were there; I just looked for the camcorders and cameras hiding behind Huntington Beach hats.

After the awards ceremony, we loaded up the van to head back to the hotel. The van burst with sweaty, blissful runners eager to shower and eat after a sizzling-hot three-mile race. Alongside us a coach drove a van filled with runners from another school. The coach pulled even to our speed and shot me an odd look. I wasn't quite sure why or what his intentions were. I responded with a friendly wave, and then my eyes wandered to the back of his van. Against the van's window, a runner held a sheet of lined notebook paper, reading, in large black letters, YOUR COACH IS A FAG. I couldn't believe a coach would participate in such a juvenile act. My athletes asked me to pull alongside so that they could display their own sign: MY COACH HAS THE FIRST-PLACE TROPHY.

The response was empowering. His athletes laughed; one even lowered his head in mock shame. We had denied them what they wanted: power. My runners loved it. They scrambled for notebook paper to write more messages. Dan held up one that said, MY COACH SAYS YOUR COACH IS A LOUSY KISSER.

The Las Vegas Invitational was just a glimpse of how good the Dynamic Duo could be. The first few weeks of the season saw them running stellar times for their age. What's more, we had developed a strong relationship with each other. Much of this bond was borne out of necessity. Athletes commonly discuss a "brotherhood" that forms from facing adversity and battling a common enemy. In short, people come together when there is a need to take up arms. Those who would have once wanted to punch each other in the nose suddenly stop bickering and work together. Coaches know that teams perform better when a high level of cohesion exists among their members. Studies show that the best method to get a team to function as a unit is to present it with a challenge. Athletes pull together, cooperate, and even bond in friendship.

At Huntington Beach we had to look no further than our own student body to find the challenge. The team bonded in a fight against adversity. After I came out, discipline problems almost entirely ended, and the team functioned as a cohesive unit.

This adversity, unfortunately, was not temporary; it didn't go away at the race's conclusion. It appeared during lunch, before and after school, even during classes. The harassment escalated during the Duo's sophomore year, especially in the locker room. We changed at the same time as the sophomore football team, the worst of the lot. The sophomore football players were convinced they were badasses. To keep up that badass image, they harassed the runners by bumping into them, slamming the runners' lockers shut, or overtly talking of the "chicks" they scored with, as if the runners weren't interested in or couldn't get girls. Without having Jon Nichols around to protect my runners, situations were often tense.

Some sophomores were worse than others. One afternoon we were running laps on the outskirts of a field. The sophomore football players were running plays, standing in line, waiting their turn. A couple of them deliberately extended the line farther and farther back, trying to get in our way without making it obvious.

I always run with my team, and I knew something about physics. An object in motion tends to stay in motion, and an object at rest tends to stay at rest. I was in motion, the football player at rest. When one of them "accidentally" backed into my path, I "accidentally" knocked him on his ass. I delighted in the humiliation he must have felt getting blown over by a flamer.

When matters escalated I hoped to rely on the administration to take care of the problem. You would think that if a student threw a glass bottle out of a moving car at a group of runners from his own school, something would happen to him. You would think that when a football player runs by the runners and calls them "Fags," he would somehow be punished. But the administrators constantly proved inept at dealing with these and other problems. Their lack of action resulted in more vocal protesting on my part. I took a paternalistic approach when it came to my runners' being harassed. But the more I dealt with the administrators, the more I realized they did not want me to bring these situations to their attention. They were not interested in disciplining those who harassed us. At one point Staunton told me, "Whenever there's a problem, you seem to be involved." I took that as a compliment instead of the accusation it was meant to be.

Even when I brought students to the administration for calling me a fag or insulting me in some other way, not much would happen. I would escort the offending student to the office, wait for an administrator, fill out paperwork, and miss whatever it was I was supposed to be doing during that time—all of this so that the administration could give the student an hour's detention or a verbal reprimand. I assure you, had these students called the principal a fag, things would have been much different. As a result of the administration's blind eye, I had to deal with these problems on my own.

The first strategy I tried in dealing with the homophobia was to act like a puffer fish, pretending to be much angrier than I truly was. I attempted to scare the other side into cessation. But I soon learned that the best way to handle these situations was not by yelling, giving suspensions, or sending them to detention but by disempowering through comedy, just as we had done with the runners in Las Vegas. If you suspend someone for calling you a fag, he will forever hate you and attach that hatred to your homosexuality. He may then grow to hate all gay men. So I decided that we were better off outsmarting them, perhaps even making them laugh.

The next time I heard an anonymous athlete yell out "Fag in the locker room!" I walked into my office, picked up the microphone, and turned on the P.A. "Excuse me?" I said. "That's Coach Fag to you."

Another time, someone from a crowded bench yelled, "You're a fag." I smirked and said, "I know that!"

It helped to have a large bag of tricks, for no two situations presented themselves exactly the same way. Knowing this, I imagined situations that were likely to happen and created witty responses to them. This equipped me to retort effectively when the real thing occurred.

As if having to battle bigots within our own school wasn't enough, we had to fight outside our school as well. Runners and coaches from other schools had learned that the Huntington Beach coach "played for the other team." This bombshell brought an onslaught of verbal harassment from other squads.

Most of the teams in our league learned of my sexuality early on; rumors about sexuality travel fast. Other coaches had to deal with my sexuality because their athletes asked questions or made comments. Some coaches chose to act as if nothing had changed. Other coaches used my sexuality as a motivational tool to get their athletes to beat mine. "You guys aren't going to let a fag team beat you today, are you?" one coach asked his team. Another yelled, "You guys are running like you should be going to Huntington Beach."

I have to laugh at coaches' attempts to motivate their athletes in such a negative way. Getting mad or psyched in distance running is a direct ticket to a poor performance. A runner needs to be relaxed and confident. A runner who views his competitors as friends is more likely to win a race than a runner who views them as enemies. Distance running is unlike football, in which you need to be tense and tight to protect yourself. The runner must be fluid, in a state of relaxed nervousness. Since emotions correlate almost directly with body tension, runners must compete as if they are in just another race; they must free themselves of psychological tension. To facilitate this, I tell runners, "It's just another race, like the dozens you've run before and like hundreds you'll run again. It's just another day in the park." It was ironic that coaches used my sexuality as a motivator, especially since they couldn't beat us. What's the point of telling athletes they're running like a bunch of fags if a bunch of supposed fags are kicking their butts?

To further counter the hostilities brought against our team, we adopted the maxim "You'll catch more flies with honey than with vinegar." I figured the best way to counter homophobes was to introduce them to a homosexual. Therefore, in the face of ostracism, we were the most hospitable team around. We invited runners from other teams to take refuge from the sun under our large shady canopy. If you needed something to eat or drink, the Huntington Beach team was the place to go. The Gastons brought food for everyone, and the Truebas brought drinks. Cheryl was sure to have snapshots she took of you from the race the week prior. And Tony and Dan were quick to point out that those photos were taken after they had already gone by. We were so gracious that the Huntington Beach canopy soon became the place to be seen. The coach could also be funny, especially when he made fun of himself. If you needed some running advice, entrance into a race, or help with an injury, you should ask Gumby, the gay coach, for help. There was always a small party around our canopy.

I also helped promote our acceptance by giving free sport psychology lectures to other teams. The lectures provided a great opportunity to befriend other coaches and athletes. Other runners soon realized that this gay guy was pretty cool, and it added a positive image to their notion of what it was to be gay. I would also bring Tony or Dan to lectures with me. Meeting a top-notch runner is a big deal to the nonelite. High school runners are praised when they dominate the county, and Tony and Dan, only sophomores, had already begun to do so. After the lectures, when we saw those runners at meets, they came over and socialized with us. Once you get a number of athletes to hang around your camp, others will as well.

We faced another obstacle besides harassment during the Duo's sophomore cross-country season: It was a low recruiting year. I received only a couple of new freshman that year, so the team size had dwindled to just nine athletes. Despite the low numbers we maintained the competitiveness for which Huntington Beach was known. In fact, the Duo led our team to a sixth-place finish in the Orange County championship race. I tried to tout the advantages of having such a small team to the runners, but they knew it bothered me. I had only been out one year and had already lost half the team. Nonetheless, I tried to focus on coaching. I put up a facade of "Everything is fine" and "I am in control." In reality, adversity was brewing.

Unbeknownst to my runners, I was having grave problems with Staunton, who informed me that Darrell Stillwagon needed to speak with me. I went to Darrell's office.

"A parent of a kid called to complain that you said you were gay and that if they didn't like that they couldn't be on the team," Darrell said.

"No, Darrell. I told them I was gay and if they didn't like that, they didn't have to be on the team."

Darrell questioned why I found it necessary to speak of my sexuality up front. I told him, "So many runners were harassed last year that I feel they have the right to know what they are getting themselves into by joining my team."

"We have 75 teachers on campus, Eric, and some gay ones, but they choose to say nothing."

"They are closeted. I am not."

"Why do you need to make an issue out of it?" he asked.

"I don't. It *is* an issue. Most of the school knows about it. They have made it an issue."

"I disagree. A black teacher wouldn't say he was black."

I laughed and said, "He wouldn't need to."

"I can see saying you're gay if students ask, but I can't believe they would ask."

"They do ask, Darrell. Daily." I looked at him with eyes beginning to narrow. "Look," I said. "If Staunton doesn't like that answer, he can speak to me directly."

Staunton constantly questioned me. Mostly he asked me about the dozens of anonymous phone calls he claimed to have received. "I got an anonymous phone call that you were seen doing this." "I got an anonymous phone call that you were seen doing that." He received so many anonymous calls about me that I began to suspect they were coming from him. Staunton was on a fishing expedition, hoping to catch something or tire me out so that I would eventually resign. Either way, it was a witch-hunt. So I watched my actions carefully.

The day after my meeting with him, Darrell told me Staunton wanted to make an appointment with me. I asked Darrell if he had told the principal why I came out to my runners.

"Yes," he replied.

"So why does he want to see me?"

"He's not satisfied with your answer."

Several days in advance, I made an appointment to meet with Staunton. At first I didn't know exactly what he was going to ask me about, but word leaked out. The athletic director told Paul Wood that Staunton had approached him about the issue and that Staunton wanted to take some action but didn't know just what. Paul leaked the information to me. Staunton was gearing for a major move.

As a child I had never been in trouble, so I had little experience at being scolded. I had never learned to deal with accusation and, therefore, internalized the fear I was feeling in the same destructive fashion in which I had hidden my sexuality. Fear permeated my conscious moments and kept me from sleeping. I imagined the worst possible scenarios. My migraines returned.

Two days before the scheduled meeting, I grew so weary of the harassment, the discrimination, the phone calls, and the inquisitions, that I decided to act before knowing exactly what to act against. When I was closeted my stomach turned with noxious feelings when I suspected someone knew I was gay; now I only got those feelings when I had to talk to Staunton. I decided that, for the first time, I would go on the offensive. I had to let him know I would not go quietly.

Anytime a problem arose between Staunton and me, I called my mother for advice. Having a judge in the family certainly eases situations such as this. My mother didn't like the sound of what was transpiring and put me in touch with one of her attorney friends—not just any lawyer but Georgia Garrett-Norris, a prominent lesbian and gay rights attorney. I met with Georgia, who said she believed Staunton was getting his ducks lined up to fire me. A day before the scheduled meeting, I informed Staunton I would be bringing an attorney to our meeting. He expressed dismay, which assured me it was necessary. If it truly were unnecessary for her to accompany me, Staunton would have had no objections. The day of the lunchtime meeting, Georgia and I walked across campus in courtroom attire.

My heart raced when we stepped into his office. Georgia calmly chitchatted with him, and then Staunton informed us that the conversation would have to be with me, not my attorney. Georgia took copious notes while Staunton and I engaged in battle.

The conversation finally shifted toward the issue at hand. Staunton began to question me, small questions at first. Finally he made his move.

"What gives you the right to tell the kids you are gay?"

I stared in astonishment. "The First Amendment."

He squirmed, flushed red, and changed tactics.

"Parents have told me you said that if the kids didn't like gays they couldn't be on the team."

"No. I said that I am gay, and if they are uncomfortable with that, they might not want to be on the team."

When it was over, Georgia asked, "Is Eric being punished or reprimanded? What's going to happen?"

Staunton's response still rings clearly in my ears. "At this point I'll have to determine whether Eric possesses the clarity of judgment to be a high school cross-country coach."

"Would this clarity of judgment be determined by the seven years of prior service before he came out of the closet or just since?" Georgia asked.

"I'll have to review my notes and get back to you."

"And I will review my notes too," she said.

Georgia and I left Staunton's office.

"Well?" I asked her.

"He's the most self-righteous, arrogant son of a bitch I've ever met!"

The week after the meeting, I waited for further developments. I worried but not to the degree I would have without my lawyer. My runners knew nothing of these proceedings. They shouldn't have to deal with it, I thought.

A few weeks later Huntington Beach High hired a new vice principal, Gary Aston, an administrator from another district. In attempt to make friends with the staff, or perhaps in a display of his convictions, Aston distributed fake money to several teachers. It was parody currency with President Clinton's picture and a caption that read "Queer as a three-dollar bill." The president was shown blowing a whistle, and the bills displayed antigay sentiments. The money's popularity with conservatives was understandable. After all, President Clinton had been talking about allowing gays in the military. I questioned the wisdom of handing the bills out at the high school, the one with a gay-straight alliance. Several teachers told me about it and wanted me to take action. So I informed my lawyer. Georgia congratulated me, telling me that if I were fired for informing the runners that I was gay under some "clarity of judgment" decision, Staunton would also have to fire the new vice principal for his "clarity of judgment." Staunton later admitted the bill distribution was "an embarrassment."

Despite all these happenings, the season had gone well. Tony, though only a sophomore, would attempt to be my first athlete to qualify for the state meet. If he did, it would be a major accomplishment. The team wasn't strong enough to make it to the prestate meet as a group, but Tony and Dan were plenty good enough to qualify as individuals. I chronicled their qualifying race in my journal:

*Tony passed by me with only a half a mile to go in sev-
enth place. The top six qualified for the state meet. "You're
doing it, Tony...one man for state, Tony...one man for
state." He soared down the final hill, moving himself into
sixth place by the bottom of the long grade. He had only to
run a quarter of a mile on the flatland to finish with his
sixth-place position and thus qualify for state. A senior with
a real strong kick, however, was pulling Tony in. I was sure
he would outkick Tony and displace him by one man.*

*The senior zoomed by Tony with blazing speed, Tony's
position sank by one, and my heart dropped to the bottom
of my stomach. Tony and I were standing on different ends
of the world. There was nothing I could do for him. He was
so far away that my voice would not even carry to him. But
I could tell he was trying to hang on to the back of the senior even though the gap between them slowly widened. I
could only hope the senior would succumb to fatigue.*

*With 200 meters left they went behind a trailer, out of
sight. When they emerged from my blocked view, Tony had
moved back into sixth place. He qualified to run in the state
meet! I cried as I ran to see him.*

Tony's run helped me attain the first of my four major goals as
a high school coach: to advance an athlete to the state meet in
cross-country. Dan missed the state meet by five spots, but he was
only a sophomore and had plenty of time ahead of him. During
the off-season between cross-country and track, I learned of a
teaching job at the adult school in our district. At adult school,
students make up credits after school or attend full-time if they are
pregnant, kicked out of their high schools, or just don't like the
environment of a regular high school. I called the school to request
permission for one of my athletes to be late to adult school. The
principal, Kerry Clitheroe, had heard of me and asked what sub-

ject I taught. I told her I was a science teacher and was looking for a job. "Really? I need a science teacher here."

A few days later I went for an interview. All went well until she told me she would be calling Staunton for a reference. I informed her that Staunton and I weren't exactly on best of terms.

"Oh, really, why?"

I explained the situation.

"Well, we have gay students here," she said. "I don't see a problem at all."

I phoned Kerry a few days later. She told me she had talked to Staunton, who adamantly opposed her hiring me. How could I find a teaching job if every employer called my principal? The only answer seemed to be to quit coaching at Huntington and become a substitute teacher in another district. That way, when the next job came up, they would call a different principal. That night I wrote in my journal:

> *I'm feeling stonewalled. How can I find a teaching job with Staunton degrading me? I'm contemplating leaving. Perhaps I could get a job as a sub in another district. Then I would have a new set of administrators to contact. At times I desperately want out of this school, but it's hard to quit on two runners as talented as the Duo. Just when I think I should move on, I watch videos of their freshman races and think about how happy I was when Ben made it to the master's meet. I want that again. Hell, they are running so well, I might not even have to wait till their senior year for that glory. Then I start thinking about how small the team is now. I need to feel important, to feel like I make a difference. I'm not teaching health, I only have nine runners on my team, and there's no improvement in sight.*

Already distressed, I did not need the phone call I received from Erich, who was now in college and an assistant coach for our team.

"Hey, Gumby, I got a message on my voice mail from the Huntington Beach Police Department."

"What about?" I asked.

"About you, Gums. They want to talk to me about you."

"Really? Why?"

"I don't know. Here, listen to the message."

Erich played the tape for me. "Hello, Erich, this is Officer Jones from the Huntington Beach Police Department sexual investigations unit. I'd like to talk to you about an accusation that has been made against your high school coach. Please call me at…" I grew instantly and overwhelmingly distressed. When I came out I suspected rumors would fly, that people would complain, that runners would quit the team. But this was more than I could handle. The fear was debilitating. I spent two days acting as normal as possible; internally, however, I was eroding. I needed to know what was going on.

Erich finally met with the detective and called me back. "Gums, somebody told the police you've been molesting the runners. He asked if you had ever molested me. I told him no, and he asked if I would tell him if it had happened, and I told him yes. He said he didn't think I should tell you."

"Who made the accusation?" I asked.

"The cop didn't know," Erich said. "It was anonymous."

I seethed at the notion of an anonymous phone call receiving such attention. If the accuser was so sure, why not stake a name to the call? And I was really growing tired of being dragged from one anonymous accusation to another. My fear, however, wasn't in being convicted, for there were no victims to come forward; my fear grew from the scarlet letter assigned to the accused. I feared being convicted by the media, having my face plastered on the front page of the paper as "accused," which today is synonymous with "guilty." Even if I evaded the press, word of the accusation would horrify parents. Reputations don't wait for court proceedings to end. This matter was potentially career ending, a reputation assassination.

I immediately called my mother. It was unspeakably painful to tell her, a judge, a respected member of the community, that the police were investigating me for unlawful sex.

My mom asked, "Did you do anything?"

"No. Nothing"

"Are you sure?"

"Mom, I think I would know if I sucked someone's dick!"

"Fine, Eric, but will anybody say you did?"

"No way."

"It doesn't matter. Trust me. People don't want to believe people are innocent of child molesting charges. You need to call Jennifer right now."

A renowned lawyer and president of the Orange County Bar Association, Jennifer Keller is experienced and connected. She tried to calm me by telling me that the police keep allegations like this quiet unless they can produce evidence. She called the detective on my behalf. His response offered no comfort.

"I talked to the detective," Jennifer told me. "He said it was a routine procedure and that he would get back to me in a few days." A few days? No words can describe the anxiety I lived through. The wait gnawed at me. Lethargy hung over me like a cloud. I couldn't for one moment clear my mind of the stress. I couldn't sleep. I couldn't even speak three sentences without the accusation creeping into my thoughts.

That night I tried to heal my wounds by running, which I had always relied on to return me to emotional balance. I laced my shoes and ran to a nearby park on a dark and dewy night. Anger pumped through my body, and I began sprinting to flush out my stress. Soon my anger turned to depression, and my pace slowed.

Tears filled my eyes. My legs grew weary, and finally I surrendered, dropping to my knees. The cold night air crept through me, and I started to shake. I collapsed onto the wet grass, curling into a defensive ball, crying, trembling.

My lawyer called a few days later. This time the detective said he had questioned several people, including a few runners, and found no truth to the allegations. "He suspects someone is trying to set you up, Eric," she said.

"What? He talked to my runners? Oh, Jesus Christ. So what now? They'll tell their parents! 'Hey, Mom, guess what? The police asked me today if Coach has ever fucked me!'"

This was fatal. Runners would talk and word would spread. Parents would pull their kids off the team, if runners didn't pull themselves off first.

"I can't take this anymore. Why the fuck can't I just coach?" I yelled, slamming my fist into the desk. "That's all I want to do. I just want to coach."

### Off-season

Weeks elapsed after the police investigation, and I waited for the other shoe to drop. I knew the legal part was over, but I desperately wanted to know what my runners were thinking. Would they withhold the information from others? Or would they assume I had actually done something and spread the word? I was afraid to talk to the runners about it because I didn't know which runners had been questioned. I didn't want to say, "Hey, Joe, did the police talk to you?"

If the police had questioned some of my athletes, I wondered why my runners had not come to me and said, "Hey, Coach, guess what?" Perhaps the police told them not to discuss it with anyone.

Every time I checked my mail, I worried I would be summoned by Staunton to discuss the allegations. I waited to find a note in my box that runner so-and-so had quit the team. Or that the *Los*

*Angeles Times* had called. I worried, stressed, and tore myself to pieces waiting for the worst. The inability to do something, anything, drained me. My days darkened by fear, I acted out my frustrations by chastising the school, the police, my job. I needed a diversion but had none. I needed friends to confide in but didn't dare. The winter months dragged into spring.

Then, from a sinking ship, a lifeboat emerged. While buying running shoes I saw a friend who coached at Saddleback College in the southernmost part of Orange County. He told me he intended to leave his position to return to school and asked if I would be interested in taking over. I stalled for a moment. Was I being offered a job as a college coach? And if I were, could I leave Huntington Beach?

"You mean give up coaching at Huntington?"

"Why not?" he asked.

Although I loved my team, the thought of escaping all the turmoil appealed to me.

"Yeah, I'm interested."

"The final decision will be up to the head track coach, John Klink," he said. "But I'll pass your name along with my recommendation. I'm not leaving until the end of track season, so you have plenty of time to decide."

I weighed the benefits of coaching at Saddleback versus Huntington Beach. Saddleback would provide a better environment for an openly gay coach, and there were other advantages too. At the collegiate level I could recruit runners who were already good. Coaching college runners would also mean not having to deal with parents, fund-raising, and the problems associated with supervising minors. The hours would be fewer, the pay better, and Saddleback is in the foothills, perfect for training.

On the other hand, if I left Huntington Beach, I would be giving up coaching the Dynamic Duo, I would have to commute 25 miles in each direction in Southern California traffic, and I would undoubtedly miss the reputation I had built at the school. The worst thought of all was that of leaving Tony and Dan. I postponed making my decision. No sense in worrying about it until I'm actually offered the position, I thought.

Three days later I got the call.

"Hi, Eric, this is John Klink from Saddleback College."

"Hi, John."

"I understand you're a top-notch distance coach," he said. "I need that here. I need someone to round out my coaching staff, and the distances are where we're lacking. Would you be interested in taking the position?"

"Yes, I'm interested," I answered. "But I have a lot to think about. Taking the job would mean giving up coaching a couple of really talented runners."

"I've heard of them. Trueba already made it to the state meet. I guess you have no complaints about that."

"They're good. And getting better all the time. That's why I'm not sure what I want to do yet."

"I understand," John said. "Come on down. Let's meet and talk about it."

So I did.

John was eager to have me coach at Saddleback. "I've heard about your success, your coaching philosophy, and about you personally," he said. "So you're a homosexual, huh?"

"Well, yes," I said. "If you want to be clinical sounding about it. But yes."

John appeared to be a stereotypical redneck. His fire-engine red face made it look as if he'd had too much to drink. He drove a truck, owned a motorcycle, and had ten pairs of blue jeans. Under his rugged exterior, however, lay a caring man. He was 50, acted 35, and sat high in the bleachers where he could bark orders to his athletes on the field below.

"Well, we don't give a shit about that here. Who you fuck is your business. As long as you're professional and a good coach, that's all that matters."

Within two weeks Saddleback College offered me the job of distance coach. But I still wasn't sure I wanted it. Or perhaps I should say I did want it but wasn't certain I was ready to leave Huntington Beach. I needed more time to think. So I phoned him. "John, I need some time to think about it," I said. "If I quit Huntington Beach, I'll be giving up a lot. I know I want to move on. I just don't want to leave Dan and Tony."

"Tell you what, Gumby, take some time, think it over, talk to some people, and let me know."

I spent a week mulling over the decision. I certainly wanted the status of being a college coach and definitely wanted to flee the rampant homophobia at Huntington Beach. On the other hand, I had an equally compelling reason to stay. I had a mission to accomplish and goals to achieve. Perhaps I was fooling myself. Perhaps I was afraid to leave the life I had established for myself at Huntington Beach despite how it had decayed. I also felt a sense of obligation to stay and finish the job I had started.

Sticking around to accomplish my goals before moving on sounded noble. Noble but foolish. To accomplish such formidable goals meant I would need more runners, and talented ones at that. I still wanted to advance an athlete to the state meet in track, to win a county championship in cross-country, and to advance my team to the state meet.

No one at Huntington Beach had ever accomplished these feats, and for years I had dreamed of being the coach to do it. Tony and Dan were seriously talented runners, and I knew, with my guidance, they would eventually advance to the state meet in track. This would secure half of my four goals. But to win an Orange County championship or make it to the state meet in cross-country would take five stud runners. And I had only two. With so few runners joining my team, the prospect of achieving my team goals looked bleak.

A week dragged by and still I had not made up my mind about the position at Saddleback. I approached Coach Wood for advice. He was noncommittal, wanting it to be my decision alone.

I then talked to Dan and Tony. Perhaps they would want me to leave Huntington Beach, thinking it was better for me, or perhaps my leaving would devastate them. We donned our rain gear, zipped up our jackets, and made our way through a dark three-mile run as rain sprinkled a soothing massage on my weary face. I still felt depressed and used the run as an opportunity to vent, discussing with them what I had thought I would not. I told them I was not as happy as when they first joined the team. I complained about the continual harassment. I expressed my dismay over the team's size. I told them about the opportunity I had at Saddleback. Then I said, "I just don't know what to do."

Dan was less emotional than Tony. He flatly stated he didn't want me to leave but added that he wanted me to do what was best for me. Tony didn't know what to say. He had always viewed me as stable, as the one who solved problems for other people. Never before had he seen me so defeated. All he could say was, "I'm sorry, Coach," as we stopped at a crosswalk. "But I'm sure glad you're here. I don't know what I would have done without you," he said in a cracking voice. "I really don't want you to go."

Tony and I had developed a deep relationship by this time. I had become like a big brother to him. When he needed help with his homework or assistance with a personal problem, I was there. He called me for advice or just to talk. I often ate dinner at his house and had become part of his family. It was mostly Tony's teary eyes, his "I don't know what I would have done without you" that inspired me to stay.

By the time I had made my decision, it was clear that nothing would come of the police investigation. There were no rumors, no scandal, no headlines, and no one had left or been pulled off the team. I called John Klink. "This was a tough decision for me, John, but I just can't give up at Huntington Beach. Not until Dan and Tony graduate."

"Tell you what," John said, "how about we make a deal? If you help me out these next two years, stop by when you can, give me workouts for the distance runners, and show up for whatever races you can, I'll hold the position for you."

"Really? You'll hold the position for two years?"

"Yes, I'm willing to wait."

"Deal!"

And with that I had a future.

I addressed the team the following day, "Gentlemen, I have been offered a job coaching at Saddleback College. I'm going to take the job but not until I'm finished here. In 2½ years you guys will be able to run for me at Saddleback, but for now I'm a Huntington Beach coach."

\*     \*     \*

More good news came when Jacob "Jake" Childs, Fountain Valley's top distance runner, phoned me.

"I want to ask you something, Coach, " he said.

"Sure, what's up?"

"Are you going to be at Huntington next year?"

"I sure am. I'll be there until Tony and Dan graduate. Why?"

"I want to run for you."

I was stunned. Jake, a sophomore like Dan and Tony, was a talented and dedicated runner. He had even beaten Dan in a freshman race the year before. Jake had always been friendly with us and sometimes warmed up for races with us. Because of this, we extended our hospitality to him and encouraged him in races. He would make a perfect training partner for Dan and Tony.

Although the thought of Jake running for us elated me, I wondered if he knew I was gay and if he knew what was happening at Huntington Beach. I figured he had the right to know what was going on before he came. If Jake wanted to transfer schools, to give up his friends and team, it was only fair he know everything. So I asked.

"You want to run for us?"

"Yes, Coach," he answered. "I want to transfer to Huntington."

"Jake, we'd love to have you, but I've got to ask you a few questions."

"Like what?"

"Why do you want to come to Huntington Beach?"

"I've thought about it since my freshman year," Jake said. "You guys are the best, and I've dreamed of being part of that. I watch the way you guys run. I see how you're all friends, and I want to be part of that too. I would've come at the end of last year, but I would've lost a year's eligibility. But with the new open enrollment rule, I can come to Huntington without losing eligibility. So I'm coming."

"That's great," I said. "Believe me, I really want you to run for us, and I know Dan and Tony would love to have you as a training partner. But are you aware of what's going on over here? Do you know I'm gay?"

"I know. I've heard the talk. I don't care. I'm cool with it. I grew up with liberal parents."

"So your parents know I'm gay?"

"Yeah."

"And they're willing to let you run for me?"

"Of course. My dad is totally excited about me running for Huntington. He's a runner too, and he's been watching the way you coach for the past year or so. Remember when you guys raced us in the dual meet last cross-country season?"

"Yes."

"I was running right there with Tony and Dan, and about halfway through the race you yelled at them 'One, two, three, *go!*' and they pulled away from me. I tried to hang with them, but they had an extra gear I just didn't have. I want you to help me get that extra gear, and my dad thinks you can do it."

I was reeling. A 16-year-old runner was talking about transferring schools to run for a gay coach!

Not minding your coach is gay is one thing, but was Jake willing to be harassed? I felt it fair that he know what to expect as a runner on our team.

"Jake, trust me," I cautioned, "I'd love to have you on the team. But I have to ask you a few more questions. Are you prepared to be discriminated against here? Are you prepared to be thought gay for transferring to my team? Are you prepared to be called a fag a dozen times a day? Are you prepared to have you car keyed? Are you prepared to go to meets and have other teams snicker at you? Because if you're not, this team is no place for you. These things happen here all the time."

"I know. I want to run for you. I've discussed all of it with my parents. I want to be on a good team. I want a real coach, and I'm willing to make the sacrifice. Besides, I've already put in the transfer papers."

"Well, then, what else can I say? Welcome aboard."

Jake would be a grand addition to the fall roster—not enough to create an awesome team; it takes five for that—but he would certainly help us win some meets. Cross-country victories are determined by adding the score of your first five finishers; the lowest score wins. You have to have five good runners to get anywhere. With Tony, Dan, and now Jake, we had three. We had a few average runners returning, but with those three up front we'd hold our own. Perhaps we would even be good enough to win a league championship.

I invited Jake and his father to my home to do a preliminary assessment of his running abilities and a psychological profile. I analyzed his running mechanics under slow motion videotape and found several inefficiencies that would need to be corrected. His dad was right; I *could* help him find that extra gear. Jake was overstriding; I prescribed for him a weekly series of five 1.2-mile uphill repeats. It's impossible to overstride when running up a hill; if you do, you'll fall over backward.

I also analyzed Jake's psychological profile. I asked him how he began running, why he ran, and what he liked most about it. I asked him to describe his best and worst race and workout. That way I could determine what type of coaching he would respond to, how he dealt with pressure, and what racing strategies would work for him. Jake was clearly bright; he had a 4.4 grade point average and produced clear, well-thought-out statements. He also possessed a desire to understand his sport.

I liked everything about Jake. He knew about subjects most 16-year-olds don't. We talked of politics, religion, and science. On top of this, Jake was good for the team. He had been coached elsewhere and had something to which he could compare our program. When he arrived he repeatedly told the other runners how lucky they were to have Erich, Harrison, and me as their coaches.

Jake's transfer to our team was great news. So was the next phone call I received, from the principal of the adult school where I had applied. To my delight, she asked me to be not only a science teacher but also the science department coordinator. The position would have medical benefits, and best of all, it would allow me to leave each day at 1 o'clock so that I could coach at Huntington at 1:30. I would no longer have to page Harrison to tell him what time I would arrive at practice.

I got Jake, I got a job, and then I got word that Tony and Dan had been entered in the Sunkist Invitational two-mile run. Sunkist, an early-season track meet, mixes high-caliber runners with indoor professional competition. To make the field you have to be excellent. Tony and Dan would be the only sophomores competing.

We arrived a few hours before the start of their two-mile race to watch the meet, hang out, and talk to other runners. As Tony, Dan, Jake, and I stood at a vendor's booth examining the latest line of running shoes, a runner from another school approached.

"Hey, Gumby. Congratulations."

"Hey, Ed. Congratulations for what?"

"Congratulations on your new runner."

How could he know about Jake transferring? I thought. Jake had just told me less than two weeks before, and he had told no one else.

"What runner?" I asked.

"Strutzel," he said.

"Strutzel?"

"Yeah, I heard Jess Strutzel is transferring to run for you."

"I think you got some misinformation."

"Well, that's what I heard, Gumby."

Jess Strutzel was a talented sprinter from La Quinta. As a sophomore he was the frosh/soph county champion in the 200 meters, the 300 hurdles, and even the 800 meters. I didn't know much else about Strutzel, and I simply passed the incident off as another rumor.

Tony and Dan ran the two-mile. Tony beat Dan with a time of 9:44, 19 seconds faster than his personal record—an inspiring time for a sophomore, especially so early in the season. Dan went out hard and paid the price, trickling to the rear of the pack and finishing second to last. Still, he tied his personal record of 9:58. Their times were favorable indicators of the forthcoming season.

After the Duo's race the meet announcer came over to congratulate us. "Thanks, Dave. It's going to be a great season for us. "By the way," I asked, "have you heard anything about Strutzel coming to Huntington?"

"Strutzel? No. How come?"

"I heard a rumor that he was transferring to my team."

"You should be so lucky, Gumby."

"Why? What do you know about him?" I asked.

"Strutzel? He's a diamond in the rough. Loaded with talent. If he lands in your hands, Gumby, it would be amazing. I'd love to see what you could do with him."

A week passed, and the first official day of track training came. I had heard nothing more of Strutzel transferring.

## Track

Coach Wood assembled the 70-plus boys into the bleachers to address them with the traditional first-day speech. He bored them with talk of conduct, expectations, and the fact that he was not their mother. After distributing the necessary forms to the athletes, who would certainly lose them between now and tomorrow, he announced, "OK, if you want to be a sprinter, go with Coach Newmire. If you want to be a hurdler, stay here. If you want to be a distance runner, go with Coach Anderson."

That was my cue to raise my hand to signal just who Coach Anderson was. I picked up my briefcase, walked across the track's infield, and into a nearby classroom. I unlocked the door and herded in the runners. I had nine distance runners, the same nine as during cross-country. I had raised my hand for nothing. There was no new blood. With a soured disposition, I launched into my own boring speech on conduct and expectations. Halfway through it, a tall, good-looking boy walked into the room.

"Are you Coach Anderson?" he asked.

"Yes."

"Hi. I'm Jess Strutzel."

Before me stood a boy whose physique modeled the running ideal. A shot of adrenaline instantly replaced my soured attitude. A huge smile deceived my attempt to hold back my energy.

"Welcome, Jess. Welcome to our team."

"Boys, this is Jess Strutzel, Orange County champion in the frosh/soph half-mile, 300 hurdles, and 200."

"Jess, this is Tony Trueba. He made it to the state meet in cross-country last season. This is Dan Gaston, the third-fastest frosh/soph two-miler in the county." I tried to keep the cool that one would expect from a seasoned coach, but the only thing preventing me from actually doing back flips was that I had not had the opportunity to talk to Jess as I had Jake. I didn't know if he knew I was gay.

Not wanting to scare him off, I decided not to tell him until he had the opportunity to get to know me.

After a round of introductions I sent the team on a warm-up and walked out to the track to talk to Coach Wood. As we watched Jess run, Coach Wood said, "You're not going to like this Eric, but Newmire wants to coach him too."

"What?"

"He's a sprinter too, Eric. He's not just a half-miler. Newmire is the sprint coach. What am I supposed to say?"

"You say 'Hell, no!' Don't let him get his hands on Jess," I said. "Don't let him anywhere near Jess. Newmire will train him to death. And while he's destroying him physically, he will demonize me."

"Look, Eric, I understand your fears, but like it or not, you're not the sprint coach."

Vexed, I turned away.

"Well, give me some time to work with him first," I said. "Don't let Newmire near him until I've had the opportunity to get to know him, till he gets to know me."

"I can do that," Paul responded.

I stood watching the team warm up. Jess's lanky stride stood out from the others. The talent Jess possessed mesmerized us. Paul saw points, first places that would help him to win track meets. I saw a heel landing. A *heel*, not a toe—the mechanics of a distance runner. Jess had sprinted some fast times, but he was obviously a distance runner by style and nature.

"Jess, come here," I said.

He ran toward me at a speed designed to impress.

"Have you ever run farther than 800?"

"Not really. I ran cross-country last year but just for conditioning."

"How'd you do?"

"Not too well," he said. "I'm pretty much a sprinter; cross-country was too far."

"Do me a favor, Jess. Run from here to the finish line at about 90% effort."

"Sure, Coach."

Jess's long legs accelerated, and he gained nearly top speed.

A heel runner! Even at this speed, he was still a heel runner. Sprinters are on their toes at that speed. Nature designed Jess to be a distance runner. And if I was correct, and if I could prove it, I could coach him full-time.

"Paul, he's a heel runner!" I exclaimed. "He's on his heels at 90% effort. He's not a sprinter. He's a distance runner."

I yelled across the track for Jess to return. This time I said, "OK, Jess, come back at 95% effort." I asked Paul to watch Jess's feet.

"Look at that. He's still on his heels," Paul said.

"Jess Strutzel is a distance runner."

"Well, he sure sprints fast for a distance runner," Paul said. "Maybe he's just a sprinter with bad form?"

"I don't think so, Paul. He's got the body of a distance runner and the mechanics of a distance runner. He's been running the wrong events.

"You could be right, Eric. Or you could be blinded by your own desire to coach him."

"Wait and see," I said. "I swear, Paul, he's a distance runner, *not* a sprinter. I want to train him for the 800 and the mile."

Paul laughed, "You want to take the county's most promising sprinter and make him a distance runner? Whether or not he was designed to be a sprinter, Eric, he's the best the county has to offer in three sprinting events. We'd be the laughingstock of the county to move him up, and we'd be foolish to give up three events for one."

"Yes, he's the most promising sprinter in the county," I said, "but he could be one of the best half-milers in the state!" I looked at Paul. "I want ten training days with him before Newmire even says hello to him. Then let me race him in the 800 and mile against Estancia. If he runs like I think he will, I'd like permission to coach him. You can run him in the sprints for the points, but I want to train him full-time."

Paul hemmed and hawed. He knew I was skilled at spotting talent and placing runners in the proper events. Several years earlier I had said the same thing about another athlete, who turned out to be one of the best distance runners we ever had. Paul also knew I was putting my reputation on the line. He slowly nodded his head. "That's fair. You train him for ten days, and we'll see how well he runs at the Estancia meet. But, Eric, if he doesn't run at least 2:03, I won't be able to justify keeping him away from Newmire."

"I know. Give me ten days, and you won't have to justify anything to anyone. Jess's legs will do all the talking."

"Good luck," Paul said.

I had ten days to win Jess over to my side and prepare him to race the 800. To do this, Jess first had to get to know and like me. If he didn't, it wouldn't matter that he was meant to be a distance runner. He would choose to sprint for the straight coach instead of running for the gay one. Second, if Jess did grow to like me, I still had to persuade him to be a distance runner. I had to convince him his other coaches were wrong to train him as a sprinter. This would be a formidable challenge, like telling Mohammed Ali he should be a wrestler.

To complicate matters, Jess would also be subjected to the same harassment as my other runners. Electing to put yourself into the middle of such strife is a decision few would choose to make, especially at such a young age. I had much to overcome if I were to coach Jess full-time.

So I went to work.

"Jess, I'd like to interview you, to discuss your past with you, and to begin to learn what makes you tick. Would you mind stopping by my house after practice?"

"Sure, Coach."

I gave him directions.

"You live on Lilac?" he asked.

"Yes," I said inquisitively.

"That's so cool. I live on the next block."

It turned out that Jess lived only a three-minute walk away. We would be able to do evening runs together, carpool to practice, and hang out more often than I could with my other athletes, most of whom lived several miles away. I conducted an interview with him and learned he was outstanding in many fields, including acting, filmmaking, and theater. He also enjoyed engaging me in lengthy debates over easily forgotten topics.

I had originally decided to mention nothing to Jess of my sexuality, but my plan didn't last long. My runners found novelty in their coach's sexuality and enjoyed discussing the issue around new runners. One of them asked, "So, Coach, what did you do last night?"

"I had a date."

"So, Coach, who was your date with?"

"Just some guy," I replied. I turned to Jess. "Did you know I'm gay?"

"Yeah, my friend Chris told me."

"You're OK with it?"

"Yeah. I think it's neat," he said.

"Neat?"

"It's unique," Jess replied. "Everybody knows who you are because of it."

"I guess so. I never thought of it like that," I said.

I grew secure in my relationship with Jess. He even told me he didn't care if others thought he was gay for being on my team. So I asked, "Are you gay?"

"No. But I don't care if people think I am. I think it's kind of neat to have people wondering."

Soon after, my trial period with Jess ended. His first 800-meter race would partially determine who would coach him. On that day his prerace nervousness grew so severe that he began to vomit. I knew from my interview with him that throwing up before races, caused by extreme nervousness, had afflicted him for years. He'd frequently vomit before, between, and after races. The problem was so severe that he was once too nervous to run a championship race. I began to work on this problem through a series of progressive visualization sessions, which served to desensitize Jess to the stress of competition.

"Get it out," I said. "You've got about ten minutes until race time. I know you feel sick now, but when the gun goes off, you'll be fine."

He vomited some more and then took his spot on the starting line. The gun fired, and Jess quickly accelerated to the lead. He ran powerfully and gracefully, and I could see the underlying talent in his form. He passed through the halfway mark well in the lead and began to open up more distance on his competitors during the second lap. Jess easily strode the final 100 meters and finished in an impressive 2:01, beating the rest of the field by six seconds. A rush ran through me as I gazed at the 2:01 on my digital watch. It was a fine race this early in the season.

I approached Jess while he stood bent at the waist vomiting—his postrace tradition, I would later learn.

"Jess, that was a great opening-season race!" I said. "You, my friend, were born to be a distance runner. Listen, I'd like for you to run the mile."

Jess looked at me in disgust. "What?"

"I want to see what you can do in the mile."

"But, Coach, (puke) I've never run (puke) the mile"

"Get it out, Jess. You have about a half an hour."

Jess's father, J.C., walked over to me. "I'm so glad you told him that," he said. "All his other coaches have just let this vomiting thing be an excuse not to run."

"Not on my team. There's nothing wrong with puking," I said. "It won't hurt him. I've already told him, 'Puke all you want, you can always make more.' If it were an injury, that's one thing, but it's just vomit. In time he'll realize that he's going to run the race whether he pukes or not. He'll get tired of it sooner or later."

Jess ran the mile and finished in third place, behind Tony and Dan—a great race for his first-ever mile. And Coach Wood was so impressed with Jess's performances that he gave me permission to coach him full-time. "By God, you were right," he said. "We'll still need him to race some of the sprints, and maybe he could do a workout with the sprinters from time to time, but you go ahead and coach him, Eric. Congratulations."

My fears of Newmire's ruining Jess had been alleviated, and his potential—not as a sprinter but as a distance runner—thrilled me. I was excited to start changing his bad habits to good ones and to transform him into a distance runner. Word began to spread throughout the county that I was going to train Jess as a distance runner, and I took a call from a reporter with the *Los Angeles Times*:

"I hear you're going to turn Strutzel into a distance runner," he said.

"That's the plan."

"You're awfully brave. Everybody thinks it's foolish."

"So I hear," I said. "I guess everyone will have to wait until the Trabuco Hills Invitational to know for sure."

A week later we ran the Trabuco Hills Invitational. Dan and Tony ran fine two-mile races at this, the first high-caliber invitational of the season. They continued to rise through the ranks of the county's finest distance runners even though they were only sophomores.

But all eyes that day were on junior Jess Strutzel. Most spectators were shocked that the county's frosh/soph champion in the 200 and 300 hurdles was no longer running sprints. Jess was up against a loaded field in the half-mile, including a 1:52 and a 1:55 half-miler, two of the best runners in the state. Jess had broken his personal record, two days prior, running 1:59, and I wanted him to drop to 1:57. I feared that the field, however, was too good for him. I worried the leaders might go out too fast for Jess, and that he would try to run with them. If he did, he would falter on the second lap. In just four curves I would either be proven a genius coach or a moronic one.

Moments before the race Jess bent over to begin his customary vomiting. But this time nothing came up. He had already begun to break the habit. He took his spot on the line, the starter raised his pistol high in the air, and a crack reverberated throughout the stadium.

Jess accelerated through the first curve, rolled off it, and found a spot in the third lane, far too wide. He ran down the backstretch in the same spot and entered the second curve still too wide, in the third lane. You don't have to be a mathematician to know that the farther you run from the curb on a curve, the farther you will run to round the corner. Jess was running farther than everyone else in the field and was doing so from the rear of the pack. He ran down the front stretch and passed two runners before hitting the halfway mark where he trailed the leaders by 30 meters. I bellowed, "Way to go, Strutzel!" But when I heard his halfway time, it was two seconds too fast. That, combined with his running the outside lanes, created a recipe for disaster.

To everyone's surprise, he entered the third curve in the second lane and began to pass runners in it. He rolled off this curve—300 meters to go—in sixth place. At this point, he entered into what we would henceforth call the Strutzel Zone. With 300 to go and 30 meters behind the leader, Jess accelerated with astounding speed.

He moved into fifth, fourth, third. With 200 meters to go he moved into second and began to challenge the leader. Jess flew past him on the final turn and sprinted home for an astoundingly shocking win. I looked at my watch: 1:53, a new meet record, a time that ranked him third in the state of California.

Never had I seen a high school 800 runner look so powerful. His time, faster by four seconds than any athlete I had ever coached, was good enough to make him one of the nation's ten best high school half-milers. My body tingled with amazement. I was so thrilled that I scaled an eight-foot chain-link fence to dash to the middle of the field and embrace my new hero.

Jess was ecstatic, and his glory showed for brief moments between puking bouts. "Jess, you're phenomenal!" I said. "My God, that's the greatest improvement I have ever seen in one race. From 1:59 to 1:53, that's amazing!" Reporters hounded him for information: "How did you improve so much?" "Why did you transfer to Huntington Beach?" "Will you give up sprinting?"

After the interviews, I sent Jess to warm down. I stood alone in the middle of the field. I had a national-caliber runner on the team, the type of runner coaches dream of but seldom get. I basked in the glory.

After meets the team always went to my house to review the videotapes of their races. Ricardo shot footage from one side of the track, while Stuart shot from the other. We watched every race twice. Today would be a unique postrace party. Tony, Dan, Jess, and all the runners had an amazing day. We had both the Strutzel Zone and Coach's magnificent scale over the fence to watch. Cars and vans crowded in front of my house. I stood at my front door, placed my key into the lock, and noticed that a strange calmness, a silence, had come over my once exuberant athletes. I opened the door, and at that moment heard a unanimous cry from my athletes, "April Fool's!"

The door opened to a Larry Flint shrine. My home brimmed with photos of nude *women*. Women everywhere! In every room they covered the walls, mirrors, ceilings, and windows. Stuart and Ricardo followed me from room to room with their camcorders catching the strange and often disgusted facial expressions I made at the sight of my statues, my busts, and even my paintings with women's breasts taped to them. My toothbrush poking through a woman's groin? They had taped photos to the ceiling above my bed, under my pillows, and even on the inside of the toilet seat lid. Barely an inch of wall did not sport a nude woman. Even the dog's water bowl had one on it. My runners had acquired a huge stack of porn magazines and spent the better part of three hours redecorating my four-bedroom house. (They had told me they were going to a movie during the afternoon break in the meet.) For days afterward, I would open a drawer and find one I missed or discover one taped to the back of a cereal box. I later learned Jess had masterminded the prank.

The gag was funny and much appreciated. I know my runners are comfortable with my sexuality when they make fun of it. It's similar to getting comfortable at a friend's house by taking your shoes off and propping your feet on the coffee table.

On Sunday I opened the paper's sports section to read the headline, STRUTZEL BREAKS AWAY. Later that day I received a call inviting Jess to compete against the nation's best at the Arcadia Invitational, a meet in which I had always wanted to enter an athlete. Jess was amazing, and he was also a distance runner.

If Jess were a distance runner, he would be the fourth quality runner we would have on our cross-country team the following fall: Tony, Dan, Jake, and now Jess. With four top runners we could do some serious damage. We would not win a county championship or advance to the state meet, but we could be very good. Jess was great for the team, but he was not the only one running well.

Tony had run an amazing two-mile for a sophomore, 9:22 on a very windy day. This performance made him the second-fastest sophomore in California. Dan had run 9:38, making him the fifth-fastest sophomore in the state.

Just as Tony, Dan, and Jess were running so well, a female student approached me to see if I would also coach her. Jennifer Spahr had bounced among five different coaches during her first two years at Huntington Beach, and she was dissatisfied with all of them. Huntington had continually hired poor coaches for its girls' team. Jennifer had begun with Dan Newmire, then bounced from one poor coach to another. I volunteered to take over the girls' program in-between each coach, but I was never given the position. I repeatedly applied for the job and was repeatedly denied. I even offered to take the position without a pay raise.

I watched many talented girls go poorly trained. I watched runners quit the team out of frustration. I just watched. Until Jennifer approached me. Her plea was so genuine, so sincere: She wanted me to coach her because she wanted to be great. I said I would have to think about it, that I would have to get the proper administrative approvals and work it out with the head girls' track coach. I was hesitant, for I knew the strife it could cause. I told her I would need time to think about it. Then I watched her race.

Jennifer was talented without a doubt. I watched her run the mile in 5:27, a good mark. A time of 5:10 is usually what it takes to get to the state meet. She had a long way to go, but she brought to mind a female Strutzel. She was running good times without quality coaching, and, above all, she was enthusiastic. In her I saw raw, untapped talent.

After Jennifer's race, I pulled her aside to talk. I gave her a modified version of the interview I give all my new athletes. I discovered how she had been training, why she ran, and how long she had been running. What her coach was doing with her was entirely wrong. Her coach was actually the pole-vault coach, and there is little similarity between the two events. He took over coaching the girls as a favor because they couldn't find anyone else. So I approached the girls' track head coach, Dana Newcomb, and asked about Jennifer working out with me.

"I've got a proposition for you," I said. "I've been watching Jennifer run. She's good, but she can be a lot better. Why don't you let her run with the boys for a while? Just a few weeks. Let me see what I can do with her. Perhaps I can get her to the state meet."

"The state meet?" Dana asked. "You think she's that good?"

"With the right training, yes. She's just like Jess Strutzel. She has talent. It just hasn't been brought out. Would you like me to give it a shot?"

"Sure, Eric, train her."

The administration wouldn't be able to stop me because I wasn't the girls' coach; I was only allowing one of the girls to train with the boys. As long as Dana had approved it, the administration could say little. Within two weeks of training with the boys' team, Jennifer dropped her mile time from 5:27 to 5:13. Pleased, Dana gave permission for her to run with us permanently.

A straight-A student, Jennifer was also the star of the visual arts department. She grew up in a no-nonsense house. Her dad was a bigwig executive for Chiquita bananas but wore blue jeans to work. Jennifer had learned from her parents to be aggressive in what she wanted. She was very attractive too and fit in perfectly with the team. She found a new training partner in Simon when I paired them for workouts. Our standard workout was 16-by-400-meter repeats—16 times around one lap hard, with a lap of jogging in-between. Simon paced Jennifer for the first ten or 11 of the repeats, and then he'd start to falter. On several occasions Jennifer ran Simon into the ground. Simon would try to push her in the repeats, encouraging her, then he would pull up with calf cramps and be forced to drop off the track. Simon even trained with her when his season ended. When Jennifer went on to compete in the championship rounds, Simon ran every workout with her.

Jess provided some intense moments as he advanced through the qualifying rounds to make his way to the state meet. Each week he ran in the same race as the nation's fastest-ever high school half-miler, Michael Grainville. He would move up onto Grainville's shoulder and try to pass him with 200 meters left. The crowds would roar as Jess battled it out with Grainville. No one had any doubt that he was a distance runner. Jess never beat Grainville, but he did push him to set another national record. I joked with Jess about how he was now trivia: "Who placed second to Michael Grainville when he broke the national high school record in 1995?"

At the state meet qualifiers Jess again placed second behind Grainville, qualifying to run the state meet. Tony and Dan fell one step short of qualifying for the state meet, but they were only sophomores. Jennifer also qualified to run in the state meet. She continued to drop her times from 5:27 at the start of the season, down to an amazing 5:00. I was correct; she was just like Jess—untapped talent. Now Jennifer was one of the fastest girls in the nation.

Jess had poor luck during the state meet. He was pushed around and tripped up, and he never recovered. He finished in last place. Nonetheless, he had posted one of the nation's fastest times the previous week, running 1:51. Sometimes in distance running it's not about who's the fastest. Racing tactics, strategies, and just plain luck often sway the outcome of the race.

Prior to this, I had only been to the state meet as a spectator. I had always dreamed of coaching an athlete in the state meet, an extraordinarily difficult task since you can only put so many people on a track. Only five individuals qualify from more than 400 schools in our section. This year Jess and Jennifer both made it, helping me accomplish the second of my four goals as a high school coach: to advance an athlete to the state meet in track.

When the season ended I sat back to look at what had occurred. I had gone from a state of deep depression to one of total elation, from questioning whether I would be staying at Huntington Beach to coaching some of the best athletes in the nation. Furthermore, the next cross-country season looked promising. Jake, Jess, Tony, and Dan were returning for the men, and Jennifer was one of the state's top returning women. I was successful as an openly gay coach. *Things can't get much better than this,* I thought, *unless we get a solid fifth man for cross-country.*

\* \* \*

A few weeks after track season ended, I was addressing the team in our meeting room when a woman entered.

"I'm looking for Coach Anderson," she said.

"I'm him."

"You're Gumby?"

"That's me."

"You look way too young to be a coach," she said.

"Thanks. I've been coaching for nine years now."

"My name is Kathy Negrete. Can I talk to you for a second?"

"Sure, let's step outside."

Outside was a runner I recognized, Jerryme Negrete from Marina High School. "Jerryme will be transferring to run for your team next year," she said.

"You want to run for us, Jerryme?"

"I do," he said.

Jerryme Negrete was Marina High School's top distance runner, just as Jake was Fountain Valley's top runner and Jess had been La Quinta's top runner. He was strong for a distance runner, larger and taller than average. He ran with exceedingly awkward form, which most coaches would use to discount his talent. Jerryme, however, ran well despite his large frame and awkward style. He was not quite as good as Jake, but he was better than any other school's fifth runner would be. Jerryme was the answer to our prayers. He was a solid fifth man.

The possibility of winning a county championship or advancing to the state meet grew from a dream to a possibility. We had five great runners, but there would be no room for error. No one could have a bad day. If they all ran well, when it counted, we could be champions.

Then reality struck. *Get a hold of yourself, Gumby,* I thought. *He's got to know what's in store for him at Huntington. It's not fair for him to transfer without knowing.* I asked to speak to Jerryme privately.

"Jerryme, I'd love to have you on our team. But I've got to ask you a few questions."

"Like what?"

"Why do you want to run for us?"

"You guys are the best. I heard Jake Childs is coming too. Is that true?"

"Yes, Jake is coming."

"I want to run for you too. We can be good, Coach."

"Yes, we can be," I said. "Real good. Believe me, I want you to run for me. I would absolutely love to have you on the team, and I know Tony, Dan, Jess, and Jake would also love to have you. But are you aware of what's going on here?

"What do you mean, Coach?"

"Jerryme, do you know I'm gay?

"Of course. Everybody knows that."

"And you're cool with it?"

"My aunt's a lesbian. It's all good."

"Does your mom know I'm gay?"

"Yeah."

"Does she care?"

"No, why would she?"

Not minding your coach being gay is one thing, but was he willing to be harassed? I gave him my standard spiel.

"Jerryme, if you come to Huntington, you are going to get a lot of harassment. Are you prepared for that? Are you prepared to be thought gay for transferring to our team? Are you prepared to be called a fag dozens of times a day? Are you prepared to have your car keyed? Are you prepared to go to meets and have other teams snicker at you? Because if you're not, this team isn't for you. All of these things happen here."

"I can handle it," he said.

I paused, then smiled. "Welcome to Huntington Beach, Jerryme!"

I brought him into the meeting room and addressed the team. "Guys, I have an announcement to make. I'd like to introduce your new teammate, Jerryme Negrete."

The team broke out in applause and cheers. "Yes!" Dan exclaimed. "Holy shit! We're going to kick ass!" The guys stood to shake Jerryme's hand. I let the runners celebrate the great news with Jerryme while I talked with his mother. That night I called Jake to give him the great news. "Jake, we have a fifth! We're going to kick butt next season!"

The glorious spring, full of delightful news and surprises, ended. We began summer training, and Jake joined us. Together, Tony, Dan, Jess, Jake, and Jerryme trained hard. We set goals for the upcoming season that included winning an Orange County Championship title and qualifying to run in the state meet.

But problems were brewing.

# Chapter Six

## The Duo's Junior Year

*Cross-country*

In high school sports in California, football is the tail that wags the dog. The powers that be use football to determine the organizational structure of almost every other sport. Meet schedules, athletic trainer schedules, stadium usage, and even the rules that govern training programs, are influenced by or modeled after the needs of football.

In the early '90s some high school football coaches were pushing their players too hard and too long during summer training. There were even a few heatstroke-related deaths. With competition for team selection being cutthroat, attendance at summer practice weighed heavily in coaches' selection of players for the fall. To protect the athletes, our local governing body imposed a "dead period" of three weeks during summer training. During this period you could not coach, but athletes were allowed to work out on their own and lift weights with a coach supervising. The rule protected the health of athletes and allowed students to take vacations without missing practices.

We make no cuts in cross-country; all who sign up make the team. A three-week dead period in cross-country helps no one and is detrimental to the runners. Distance runners cannot take three weeks off at the onset of the season. If they did, they would lose months of aerobic conditioning, which could result in injury during the fall cross-country season. I jokingly called the dead period the "follow-it-and-you're-dead period." Thus, nearly every coach who cared about his athletes had to work the system, bending, without breaking, the rules. The rules didn't prevent the athletes from running; they merely prevented the coach from coaching. Thus, some coaches swapped duties and coached at each other's schools, while others were absent from practice but ran the program with their team captain. Some coaches ran practice through another organization, such as a community-based running club. This was the method I chose.

I created my own community-based cross-country running club. Darrell Stillwagon had given me the idea years earlier. "As long as they're not meeting under the guise of Huntington Beach High School and they're not using the school's facilities, it's OK," he said. For years during the dead period, the club met at my house or some other location besides the high school. The past summer had been no different. The club met at my house for three weeks every other day, for a total of ten days. The new girls' coach followed my lead and did the same with her team, except for Jennifer, who trained with us. The girls' coach thought it beneficial for Jennifer to train with the boys, as she had done the same in college to maximize her own ability.

After the dead period ended and school began, I retrieved a memo that read, "See Jim Staunton regarding summer training." Anxiety hit me, so I knocked on his door moments later. He invited me into his office, then questioned me about our summer training during the dead period. "A concerned grandparent has complained that you're having mandatory practice at your home," he said.

I explained to him that it was not a Huntington Beach practice but my own club, and, as such, could not possibly be mandatory. I explained that Darrell Stillwagon had approved of the plan. I also informed him that this was a common practice among coaches and that the girls' team had done the same. Staunton, nonetheless, decided that since I had been involved, and that athletes from Huntington Beach had participated, it was illegal.

"Effective today," Staunton said, "and for a period of ten coaching days, I am suspending you."

I sat silently for a few moments, then decided to find out what constituted a suspension before trying to fight it.

"Exactly what does this mean?" I asked.

"For a period of ten training days you will not be allowed to coach. I will also have to call the California Interscholastic Federation and let them know I discovered a rule violation and will be punishing you."

"OK, but during that time the team planned to sponsor a road race to raise funds," I said. "We're also set to attend the Las Vegas Invitational." I paused and thought a moment. "If I can't coach, what do I do about supervising practice? Will you be getting a substitute?"

"I guess it would be appropriate for you to attend practice, for supervisory purposes, but you are not to coach while you are there," Staunton responded.

This would take care of the three school days left that week, but the fourth day was a Saturday, the day we were sponsoring a community race as a fund-raiser.

"Just supervise the fund-raising," he told me.

The next school week would involve more supervising practice, and the final day of the suspension fell on the day we were to leave for the Las Vegas Invitational.

"Don't coach them. Just supervise their transportation and lodging," Staunton said.

That's not so bad, I thought. I would be doing the exact same thing I normally did, except I would call it supervising instead of coaching. I left Staunton's office feeling as if the whole thing was pointless.

I called my lawyer that evening. Georgia informed me, "Since the girls' coach was not punished for committing the same violation, the fact that she wasn't even questioned is a clear case of selective enforcement. Selective enforcement is a form of discrimination."

She continued, "The question at hand is not whether you actually broke a rule. The question is why the principal is selecting you, and you only, for enforcement of that rule. It's no different than a cop who pulls only black drivers over."

I consulted several coaches who all agreed. I could push the issue and certainly win. The principal had no legal basis to tell me whom I could or couldn't coach on my own time. Case law, I knew, supported me; our governing body had lost a court case with a swim coach over the same issue.

I could make a stand, but the procedure for fighting administrative actions required the coach be placed on temporary suspension until the matter was cleared. To clear such a matter would have undoubtedly taken far more than ten days. I also realized that Staunton was not pushing the issue very hard. He could have been more aggressive but wasn't. Perhaps he used the dead-week issue as bait while fishing for something else. If so, he caught nothing. But the situation served as a nice warm-up for what occurred immediately upon my return from suspension.

I retrieved another summons from Staunton. I got so many notes to see him that I had learned to avoid checking my mail on meet days, knowing that finding a note would sour my attitude and affect my runners' performances. On the other hand, if I didn't check my mailbox, I maintained a low-level anxiety, a similar feeling to awaiting the results of a medical test.

The note informed me that I was being charged with illegally recruiting Jake Childs. Staunton grilled me about him and under what circumstances he had decided to transfer. I was furious. Jake had done everything properly and had contacted the administration before talking to me. All Staunton had to do was ask Stillwagon. Furthermore, Jake had turned in his paperwork eight months ago. Why would charges arise now?

Jake had taken advantage of a new rule. In the past if an athlete transferred to another school, he lost a year's worth of athletic eligibility. After the rule was changed, allowing athletes to transfer without penalty, Jake took advantage and submitted his paperwork. One major stipulation is that the athlete must make first contact with the new school. This was most certainly the case with Jake, who had initially contacted Stillwagon. He had talked to Stillwagon and turned in his paperwork even before he had called me. I told Staunton this.

Nonetheless, Staunton said, "I have to look into these charges, and I will need to interview both Jake and his parents."

Jake discussed the issue with his parents that evening, and they wrote the following letter to Staunton:

> *Jacob started running his freshman year at Fountain Valley High School. He loved running and was looking forward to the cross-country team. What we found was that the Fountain Valley program was a joke. The coach was present only at the start of practice, and we were amazed that the team never warmed up before a race. The boys would sit under a tree until they walked to the starting line. There was no team camaraderie, and we would watch with envy as the Huntington Beach team would warm up together, stretch together, and even warm down after the race. We hoped things would get better his sophomore year but they did not.*
>
> *The turning point came at the Trabuco Hills Invitational when Jacob's coach asked us to write down Jacob's time for*

*him because he couldn't stay. We were puzzled. How is it a
coach is unable to stay to watch his number 1 varsity runner's
event? Jacob is thankful he made the decision to transfer
when he did. He made this decision independently and with
no discussion with Coach Eric Anderson. When Jacob
informed Coach Anderson of his plan to transfer, the coach
told him to think it over carefully. He counseled him he
would be leaving longtime friends and should discuss it fully
with his parents before making an irreversible decision.
Jacob was never, in any way, recruited.*

    *There always seem to be those who find it easier to crit-
icize excellence, rather than to seek it themselves. Instead of
penalizing the runners, we should be commending these
fine young athletes and their coach and celebrating their
exceptional achievements.*

*Robert F. Childs*
*Sue Ellen H. Childs*

The Childses were understandably upset, since they had done
everything properly. They had even discussed Jake's transfer with
Fountain Valley's principal, a move they didn't have to make.
Acting considerately, they kept the transfer quiet until Jake's final
season at Fountain Valley had ended, at which time Jake told the
coach in private and even wrote him a letter of gratitude.

The illegal-recruiting accusation was in no way deserved, and
considering how properly the family had acted, and that Sue Ellen
Childs was still volunteering her time at Fountain Valley, the accusation was downright rude. She was so mad, she met with the
Fountain Valley principal to discuss with him just how insulting it
was that they could do everything precisely as they were advised
and then be charged with these allegations. Jake's parents took care
of everything. I did nothing, and the matter was soon dropped.

In the Fountain Valley coach's mind, however, the matter was not cleared up. Another visit to my mailbox brought another memo, a rap on Staunton's door, false salutations, and an accusation of illegally training my runners by having them practice with Saddleback College. The charge was made anonymously, but evidence pointed to the disgruntled Fountain Valley coach as the accuser.

After telling John Klink I would not leave Huntington Beach until the Dynamic Duo did, I had promised to help him in the meantime. When schedules allowed, I sometimes coached both teams on the same day. Even though a coach may work for both a high school and a college team, it's illegal for high school runners to train with a college team. Occasionally, Klink's team trained in the same location as mine, so I could coach them when I was done with my team. One day I coached the Huntington Beach runners, finished, and sent them home. As they left, the Saddleback van pulled up and its runners emerged. There was a one-minute overlap when my runners were leaving and his runners were arriving. Enough time for them to say hello to each other, but no one ran together. After the Huntington Beach team left, I coached the Saddleback team. The anonymous caller gave the exact time and location of the incident, and the only other team out there that afternoon had been Fountain Valley.

I carefully explained to Staunton the circumstances of that day and stated that no simultaneous training had taken place. As usual, he was not satisfied. He fished for more.

"Have you ever trained together?" he asked.

"No."

"Have any of your kids trained with Saddleback?"

"No."

"Have any of Saddleback's runners trained with ours?"

"No."

Staunton ended the inquisition early this time. "OK, Eric, but I must warn you that training together is illegal."

"I'm well aware of that," I said.

Subsequent visits to my mailbox summoned me to meetings with Staunton regarding anonymous accusations of other training violations. One caller claimed I was coaching on Sundays; another maintained I'd illegally recruited Jerryme Negrete. And these are just a few examples. None of the charges was valid, but each gave Staunton the opportunity to question me about a variety of other matters. It was like a living chess game. It was stressful at first, but after so many accusations I began to grow desensitized to them. Eventually, even Staunton began to ignore them.

One allegation was quite comical. Staunton received a complaint from a local business owner that I had entered her business and created a disturbance, causing customers to leave the store. In reality, a kid had joined the team with the intent of evading P.E. He actually had little interest in running, coming up with daily excuses as to why he couldn't run. One day he forgot to bring his running shoes, so I told him to wait in the library so that he would be supervised until we returned from practice. I checked the library ten minutes later, and he was not there. Someone told me he had gone to the comic-book shop across the street, so I went there. Sure enough, he was there reading comic books. I walked over to him and said, "Turn in your gear in tomorrow. You're off the team." I left before he could say anything.

But this wasn't the story Staunton heard. "The business owner says you walked into the store and yelled loudly at the student, 'I don't care who your mother is; nobody can touch me. I'll have your mother shut up if she says anything.'" The store owner also told Staunton that the store's employee concurred with the story. Making matters worse, the mother called too. Things didn't look good for me, as it sounded as if I'd made death threats to the student's mother.

Staunton questioned me at length and then called the store owner for more information. Slowly the truth emerged. Finally, even Staunton laughed when he learned the business owner was not in the store at the time of the "incident" and that she had only heard about it from an employee. And who was the employee? The kid himself. He had been working at the store during school hours.

Despite the numerous accusations, the team went undefeated for six weeks. Both the talent and character of our runners contributed to our successful record.

Jake proved a remarkable addition to the team. He could break the thickest prerace tension with one flash of his bright smile or the comic relief of an amusing comment. He also helped his teammates deal with other teams' snickering and name-calling. He handled adversity well and became the glue that held the team together.

Because we were a motley crew, creating a cohesive family was difficult. Jess was somewhat like Jake: He was gregarious and enjoyed intellectual conversations. Tony and Dan, however, were talkative on more prosaic issues. Jerryme marched to an entirely different drummer. He was strictly into "chicks, cars, and music."

Despite this mixture, Jake possessed a wizardry that enabled him to, as Kipling said, "walk with kings" but not "lose the common touch." He was instrumental in the team's functioning and became everyone's confidant. He was also the first to provide a congratulatory hug or consoling arm around the shoulder, and he wasn't afraid of being perceived gay for it. When Jake was at Fountain Valley, his teammates would not permit this kind of physical affection. He wasn't welcome to hang on their shoulder or provide a postrace hug. Homophobia limits acceptable behaviors for males. On our team, however, restrictive notions of masculinity were nonexistent. Gone was the posturing that robs a man of his ability to share intimately.

In races, Jess, Jake, and Jerryme added great support to the one-two punch Tony and Dan provided. As the season progressed. I grew convinced we could win the Orange County cross-country championship, a feat Huntington Beach had never accomplished. We were often in the top ten but never better than fourth.

Orange County has many strong teams for a variety of reasons. First, Orange County has more than 60 high schools, averaging about 1,500 students each. We also have perfect weather for distance running. We can run in shorts and T-shirts year-round. Additionally, our schools used to pay our teachers relatively well. There was, therefore, no reason for teachers to leave our schools to seek higher wages. Orange County brimmed with coaches who had put in 20 years or more. After coaching for that long, you cannot help learning a few things that make you a better coach.

These factors created fierce competition for the Orange County championship. This was the first year I thought we could win it. The week before the race I spent hours working out strategies, determining how I thought other teams would race and which runners would break up our scoring. Should my faster runners slow down to help the slower ones place better? Should we run as individuals? Should we go hard from the gun or start off easy and work through the field? I called upon my years of coaching to recall how fast the lead pack normally ran, and I averaged the scores from previous years to see how many points were needed to win. After considerable analysis, I devised a plan I felt would best enable us to come out on top. But before I could inform the team of my strategy, I received a discouraging phone call.

I had been coaching track and cross-country a long time; I should have known better than to make such a mistake. In cross-country each athlete is allowed to compete in only 11 seasonal races before the championship rounds. It doesn't matter how many races the team runs, as long as each runner competes in no more than 11. If a runner exceeds the number of races allotted, he is disqualified from the championship rounds of competition. I had scheduled my top varsity runners for 12 races instead of 11.

A friend called to inform me of the mistake before I had actually violated the rule. We had two meets remaining and could only run one of them. We would either have to scrap a dual meet against Edison or withdraw from the Orange County championship meet. The choice was a no-brainer. The dual meet was inconsequential. If I pulled my top runners and our team lost, it would just add one meet to our loss column. We'd still run the meet, but we'd keep our top men out of it. That way, we could run the county championship race and violate no rules in the process.

Hoping to handle the situation with professionalism and dignity, I called my athletic director, explained the mistake, and told him I would hold my top runners out of the dual meet. He told Staunton, who proceeded to question me about it. I have no idea why, because a coach has every right to choose what races his athletes run.

I also called Edison's coach and informed him that we would be holding our top-notch runners out of the dual meet race. Although there was no rule requiring this, I thought it considerate to let him know so that he would not have to prepare his athletes for a tough race that day.

My consideration, however, was not met with equal respect. Edison's coach saw an opportunity to smear my program and jumped on it. Perhaps he sought revenge. The year prior he had tried to recruit Jake (illegally) to run for him rather than Huntington.

The day after talking to Edison's coach, I answered a call from a *Los Angeles Times* reporter who asked for my version of the story. "What?" I asked. "You guys are doing an article on this? Are you sure it's even newsworthy?"

"You're the top-ranked team in the county," the reporter said, "and Edison's coach thinks you're making the wrong choice. He says you're doing it to spite them and that you're being untrue to your league."

I offered the reporter my version and awaited the results. HUNTINGTON BEACH AND EDISON BATTLE OFF THE TRACK, the headline

read. The story began with Edison's allegations but by the end
suggested it was a case of sour grapes for Edison. I ran our second
string against Edison's first, and they beat us badly.

On Friday, the day before the county meet, I drew the three-mile
course on the chalkboard and explained my strategy. I gave each runner a specific duty, a responsibility to uphold. Some athletes were given
conservative race plans; others were told to gamble. I figured we could
win the title by as much as ten points. I also devised a race plan for
Jennifer, who would be attempting to prove herself as the fastest junior in the county. The runners left the room confident. My plan was
now our plan, and their execution would determine the outcome.

We met at the high school before dawn and drove to the race.
My runners knew not to talk about the race that morning.
Experience had taught me to talk about other topics and to have a
good time, rather than stress about the race. Inside, however, we
each knew this day was momentous.

My runners wanted the title for the sheer glory of it. I shared
their passion for glory but wanted it for a different reason. To me,
winning the county title would mean I had succeeded as a gay
coach. I wanted to prove that openly gay coaches could be great
coaches, even in a conservative county. If I could be the best in
Orange County, I would send a message to closeted coaches everywhere that they too could succeed.

More significantly, I desired the victory for the dozens of closeted gay athletes who would watch us win. I envisioned a freshman, closeted and afraid, experiencing the same turmoil I had at
that age. I saw him sitting among his teammates at the award ceremony, taking secret pride in what our team had done. I wanted
this title, on this day, more than anything else.

The prerace anxiety was greater than I had ever experienced. A
dozen top-ranked teams stretched across the width of the street,
which would quickly narrow to half its original width. The race
would start with a furious scramble for position before the road

narrowed. The cacophony of several hundred onlookers fueled our nervousness, and a colony of butterflies made residence in my stomach.

"Stay calm, boys. Follow the plan." I said as I massaged the shoulders of each runner moments before the start. "Relax. Relax," I reminded them, then left the team and stood on an embankment to take an aerial view of the start. The gun sounded, elbows flew, and a runner in the field went down. *Please don't let it be one of mine.* I counted my boys as the field returned for a second start. *Five...six...seven.* My boys were all safe. But some poor runner from another school had broken his arm in the fall. Again the runners took their spots on the starting line.

The second start of a race is always more chaotic than the first. Everyone who got a good start does precisely what he did before, and everyone who got a poor start goes out faster in an attempt to do better. Our boys knew they had to sprint the first 80 meters to avoid being pushed to the back.

As the second gun sounded, the crowd sprinted toward me. As the boys passed I read the names on the backs of our white jerseys to determine their position. Trueba, Gaston, Childs, Strutzel, Negrete—all five were in good position. My harriers were off chasing our dreams. I jumped from my viewing point and scrambled across a dried streambed to see them at the .75-mile mark.

Our strategy could be simplified into the following: Gain a start in the front of the pack so that everyone sees we're going for the victory, then slow the pace throughout the duration of the first mile, making it appear we had gone out too hard and were dying. Doing this would sucker other teams into thinking they could beat us, inspiring them to run too hard up the first major hill. This would fatigue them, and we would then begin to retake our lead. In short, we were tricking them into running too hard too soon.

Our runners did as instructed, and at about the .75-mile mark, I heard other coaches yelling, "Huntington Beach is out of it!

Huntington Beach is out!" *Perfect!* I thought. This was just before the major hill. Surely other teams would surge now—at exactly the wrong time. Meanwhile, I called to my runners, "The plan is working. Have faith. It's working."

The plan was risky, but it was our best chance. I gambled on a working knowledge of how other teams' runners would react, but I also gambled on my own runners. My runners would have difficulty following the plan, since Tony and Dan usually ran from the front, not from behind. Asking them to run from the rear of the race was like asking a bird to walk rather than fly. They'd want to take off, to assert their strength. To contain these emotions, to refrain from acting on instincts, runners must have a great deal of faith in their abilities. It discourages them to see so many others in front of them during a race when they're used to seeing only a few.

Still, if a runner believes in his coach's plan and his own abilities, he can use these people as inspiration when he passes them in later stages of the race. I planned for my runners to make their move when the others were weakened, which meant we would start to move up right after the first major hill, shortly after the mile mark. We would then work through the field, pulling runners in one by one, until we reached the 2.5-mile mark at the top of the final hill. From there, it would be a half-mile downhill sprint. We planned to take the title during this last half-mile, to steal it at the last moment.

After my runners passed the .75-mile mark, I darted back across the dried streambed to see them hit the 1.5-mile mark. A wall of people lined the course at the 1.5-mile mark, cheering the runners along a 300-meter section. I stood at the end of the wall, unable to see the runners until the end of this stretch, but I could hear the crowds cheering the leader.

Soon the spectators stepped out of the way to reveal the race leader. He wore a white jersey. His form looked familiar, and a large HB came into focus. Tony was leading the race. He had a five-second lead over second place. Although this was exciting, I knew the other boy was usually strong during the last mile of his races. By no means had Tony secured a victory. Another ten seconds behind that runner was a large pack of 30 or 40 runners. In it were many runners from the top teams, but none from Huntington Beach. Our runners trailed the pack, and I figured our team position to be approximately fourth. They had moved up about eight spots since I last saw them, and I hoped they would continue to advance.

Our team looked strong, and I grew excited. As our top five runners passed, I yelled, "The plan is working. We're moving through the ranks." I then scurried up the side of a steep hill to make my way to the last half-mile, where we had planned to steal the show.

I stood with a half a mile to go, waiting for our runners to come over the hill. I hadn't seen them in a few minutes and hoped they had continued to advance through the ranks as planned. The far-off crowds began to cheer the first runner cresting the top of the hill. The spectators again spread apart, revealing the faint outline of the race leader. Cresting the top of the hill was—it looked like—a white jersey. It was still Tony! Waves of euphoria surged through me as Tony led the field. "Way to go, Tony!" I exclaimed. "County champion, Tony! You're going to be county champion!" Tony ran by me, outdistancing second place by nine seconds. He would undoubtedly be the individual overall county champion. I began to cry from joy before the race even ended. Even if we didn't win as a team, this was a major accomplishment. No Huntington Beach runner had ever won the race.

I turned my attention back to the rest of the race and counted six other runners before my next hero emerged. It was Jess Strutzel, running the race of his life. "Way to go, Strutzel!" Jess had moved up from around 40th and was now in eighth place. So many coaches had told me he wouldn't be able to run three miles.

"He's just a short distance runner," they said. Jess was proving he was whatever the hell he wanted to be.

Dan was close behind Jess, and soon to follow was Jake. Jerryme wasn't supposed to be near them, and he wasn't. I headed to the finish before I saw Jerryme. I knew we looked good with the top four men, but I would have to wait to see where Jerryme was to determine which place we were actually in.

I careened down the side of the hill and made my way to the finish line just in time to watch Tony barrel down the final winding path. To the tune of hundreds of cheering fans, Tony ran away with the title. A shot of adrenaline surged through me as his arms rose victoriously in the air. I pushed my way through the crowds, spotted my sweat-soaked hero, and congratulated him with a hug. In rushed excitement, we turned to watch the others finish. Second, third, fourth, fifth, sixth, and seventh places emerged, then Jess rounded the corner. With only 200 meters left, in front of hundreds of energized fans, Jess found his zone. He pulled out a remarkable kick. "Jesus Christ, look at Jess go!" Tony exclaimed, "He's gonna get 'em all." Jess kicked past seventh, sixth, fifth, and right at the finish line he stole fourth place. He hit the line, and his arms shot straight to the air in elation.

Jess made his way to Tony and me, and the three of us embraced. Jess's wide smile almost prevented him from saying, "Did you see that?" He then broke into laughter at his own amazement. "Jess," I exclaimed, "You're the first senior in the county to finish. You're the senior county champion!" Jess, the senior class champion, and Tony, the junior class champion and overall champion, waited apprehensively to see if we could win the team title as well.

Two white singlets rounded the corner in stride. I saw HB, which signaled Jake and Dan, in 17th and 18th place. This was good, about where they were supposed to be. Meanwhile I observed the finishers from other teams. They placed as I expected them to, meaning it was up to Jeremy to win. Thus far, everyone had done his job. We needed just one more. Our fifth man held the team's fate in his hands. Jerryme would need to finish in the top 40 for us to win the title.

The 29th and 30th runners passed, 31, and...then...Jerryme! My arms shot up, each hand holding up just one finger, signifying victory to my runners, their parents, and all our alumni who had come to watch Huntington Beach win their first-ever county title. We, the assumed gay team, and I, the gay coach, were champions.

Jerryme hit the finish line, and my ecstatic runners clamored to hug and congratulate each other.

I felt tremendous pride. My runners got what they had come to Huntington Beach for: glory. Shortly after their race ended, Jennifer earned her glory. Fueled by the success of her male comrades, Jennifer ran one of the best races of her life. She careened up and down the hills while the boys scrambled along the course cheering. When she emerged at the top of the final hill, it was clear she would be Orange County's fastest junior runner. Jennifer crossed the finish line to be crowned the Orange County junior-class champion and overall runner-up.

Tony was both the junior-class champion and the overall county champion. Jess was the senior-class champion and the third runner-up overall. And our team won the Orange County championship.

I had accomplished three of my four goals: to advance an athlete to the state meet in track, to advance an athlete to the state meet in cross-country, and to win an Orange County Championship title in cross-country. Several years later, as I look back on that day and that victory, I realize it brought with it all I had hoped it would. I have since talked to three closeted runners who were in the audience that day—young men like Ryan, whom I met two years later on the Internet.

"Are you the coach at Huntington Beach?" Ryan typed.

"I used to be."

"You're the gay one, right?"

"Yes."

"I was so happy when you guys won the Orange County championship title a few years back."

Ryan was only a sophomore when he watched us receive our trophy. He knew he was gay and wished he could have run for a team like ours. Instead Ryan ran for a Catholic school. Today he is out of the closet and happy.

With our county title I had one major goal left: to qualify a team for the cross-country state meet. In contrast to how we looked a year ago, this year we were in good position to achieve that goal. But we first had to advance through the necessary rounds to gain way to the state meet.

The importance of our league meet was inflated in the press because of the awaited showdown between Edison and Huntington. The showdown was trumpeted, but the results were played through a kazoo. Tony won the race, Dan came in second, Strutzel came in third, and we stomped Edison. The next week, at the CIF preliminaries, we placed an impressive second and easily advanced to the state preliminaries.

In the state preliminary meet 12 strong teams from Orange, Los Angeles, Riverside, and Ventura counties compete. Only four of these teams advance to the state meet. Huntington Beach had never finished better than sixth, but we entered the meet this year with our best team ever. Ranked third, we would have to fall a long way to land in a nonqualifying spot. I felt confident we would, for the first time, advance as a team to the state meet. I had set my hopes on it since this would be my last chance. After this year Jess and Jerryme would graduate, and no one on the current roster had the talent to replace them. With no transfers on the horizon, it was my final chance.

It's astounding that you can train flawlessly for a year, and then, in one critical moment, your dreams are smashed. That is the brutal nature of sport. You must be faultless in your preparation and your execution, or you must wait another year.

Normally we would run a specific warm-up route and then go into our stretching regime. But on this race morning, Jennifer was racing before us. I wanted my boys to cheer her on and warm up for their race at the same time. You can't have it both ways. I was ambiguous in my instructions. I didn't give my runners clear and precise directives. I shouldn't have broken the routine. You never try something new on the morning of a big race.

During the warm-up my runners grew confused about what to do. In an agitated state, they argued among themselves and eventually separated in anger. After Jennifer's awesome performance, in which she qualified for the state meet, I returned to our camp to find the boys finishing their stretching program. They were quiet, not talking and laughing as they usually were. Tony's face revealed something very wrong.

With just three minutes before the race, I could do little. The Orange County champions entered the race in an angered state, and we fell to sixth place, two spots out of qualifying position for the state meet. Even worse, none of the boys qualified individually. It was a disgrace. It was my fault. Later that week I wrote in my journal:

> *The embarrassment, the anger, the humiliation I could do without. The sadness, though, for this I am glad. For if I were not as depressed over this race as I was, it would have meant we weren't as good as we were—and we were good. It is only now, days after, that I can even write about the race.*

Depressed in Fresno, the night before Jennifer ran the California state meet, I browsed through a Barnes and Noble bookstore. Sipping an overpriced mocha, I passed a batch of books and the word *runner* caught my eye. The blue cover sported the title *The Front Runner*. Scores of fiction readers had recommended it to me.

I had always responded, "I don't read fiction. I'd much rather read a textbook, something I can highlight as I go along." Nonetheless, in a momentary lapse, I bought an autographed copy.

Jennifer ran exceptionally well in her first California cross-country state meet. Her time was good, and several college coaches approached her after the race, including one from Stanford. I treated her to a victory lunch, but for me the celebration and the whole trip lacked joy. The deep depression of our team's not qualifying for the state meet stuck to me. I was exuberant for Jennifer, but I couldn't help feeling I had let down my boys—and myself.

Each year, after the conclusion of cross-country, I grew depressed. I attributed this to missing the thrill and even the anxiety of coaching. I missed the companionship and interaction with the team. This, combined with the short, dim, rainy days of winter, fueled my depression. Still sick with depression from our great flop, I quickly felt the darkness take hold. Facing a five-hour trip home, I asked Harrison, my assistant coach, to drive while I read the book I had purchased the night before.

At first I read with speed, simply trying to get through the novel so that I could get to the more important stack of books waiting at home. I read the story of Harlan Brown, a gay coach at a premier distance-running university. His sexuality is discovered, he is jeered, his name blackened. He is forced to abandon his dreams of coaching the cadre of distance runners and takes refuge at a small liberal arts college where he coaches lesser athletes. The master coach is reduced to P.E. instructor.

Although he longs to coach at a higher level, he is unable to recruit top athletes. Then, on a rain-darkened morning, light shines upon Harlan Brown. Three of the nation's finest distance runners seek his coaching. Rumor has it that the boys were ousted from their previous university for disciplinary reasons.

"Why would I want to take on three discipline problems?" Harlan asks.

The runners reply, "That's their version. Would you like to hear ours?"

Harlan leans back in his chair and says, "Go on."

"We're gay."

The artistry with which Patricia Nell Warren crafted the novel evoked a response I had never felt from fiction. *The Front Runner* was alive in me and is partly responsible for my desire to write this book.

I was eager to meet the author. At least one person could empathize with what I'd been through. What's more, she happened to be a lesbian. I closed the book, wiped my tears, and wrote her a note. She soon responded: "Your letter has me reeling. I have received hundreds of letters from people relating to Billy, but you are the first who relates to Harlan. You are a true Harlan Brown."

A few weeks later I met the liveliest lesbian ever. Patricia is an ardent gay rights activist, and before long she hooked me into a network of writers and activists. I was invited to speak on panels, to conferences, and in classes. I began a new period in my life, one I had never expected, that of an activist.

Involvement in the gay community helped me ward off depression. I began working with Patricia on several gay youth events and began organizing people in Orange County. I also spent some time doing what everyone says not to. I looked for a boyfriend, and I found one.

Mattias was a gorgeous 21-year-old student from Sweden who possessed a thick accent that melted me. His tall, slender, and well-defined body took the form of a runner. Yet he had no interest in sports. Mattias was fascinated with the arts—interests far different from mine. He also spoke three languages and was learning two others. He danced, drew, and created art from a variety of mediums. Usually preoccupied with science, athletics, and social sciences, I was now alive with the sense of beauty of a fine artist. I remember the moment I fell in love with him.

The feeling began early in the evening as we dined aboard the Queen Mary in Long Beach. Afterward, we strolled along the outer decks of the ship and found a private area on the aft where Mattias imitated a tap-dancing sailor from a Fred Astaire musical. We then prowled the lower decks (posted off-limits), gaining entry into the darkened engine room. Later we peeked through a door that opened into the grand ballroom, a beautiful wooden floor and exquisite tapestries adorning its walls. Mattias took my hand and led me in a waltz around the dance floor. My two left feet scrambled to keep up with the rhythm of his refined movements. Unable to maintain the fervid pace, I began to laugh. I shook my head as Mattias pulled me into another round of dance. Our eyes caught, I drew him in, and we shared our first kiss in the middle of the dance floor in the elegant ballroom.

We returned to his student-budget apartment, and he played his rented piano in a room with just enough light to cast lonesome shadows. Idle from an evening of wonder, I lay on a couch he could have only bought from a thrift store. I watched his graceful movements. His head bobbed and swayed with the rhythm of his notes. The tranquilizing music, soft and melodious, paralyzed my body, preventing me from catching my falling heart. After he finished playing the piece, Mattias turned to me. "Did you like it?"

"Beautiful, Mattias. Simply beautiful. What was it?"

"I have not named it yet."

*Off-season*

In the winter Cupid went crazy. Romance found others too. Tony found his first long-term girlfriend, a runner from another school. He had dated a few girls, but this was his first serious relationship. Interestingly, Mattias was my first real boyfriend as well, and I was 27! Jennifer found a boyfriend, a runner from Marina, the brother of the coach, in fact. Jake found love in the arms of a strikingly good-looking girl who lived 60 miles away. And Jess? Jess never had girlfriends, just girls he dated: He kept his mystique by never calling them girlfriends. Many of us fell in love, and within the first few weeks of the next track season, we all fell out of love, including me. Love and track don't seem to mix.

The team looked stronger than ever. We had Tony, Dan, and Jake in the mile and two-mile, Jess and Jerryme in the 800, and Jennifer in the mile and two-mile. I looked forward to again making the state meet, but this time with two or more athletes.

I headed to check my mail one afternoon, to see if any more ridiculous complaints had been lodged, and in my box I found a note: "See Mr. Staunton." I rapped on his door and was presented with unexpectedly bad news. No allegation or accusation from the outside on this one; this time we were attacked from within. The head girls' track coach, Dana Newcomb, who had given permission to train Jennifer the previous year, decided Jennifer could no longer run with the boys.

One would think the administration would support her running with us. We had helped her become one of the top runners in the state, and with that improvement came scholarship offers. Best of all, Jennifer had dreamed of attending Stanford, and, after her Orange County championship win, they had offered her a scholarship contingent upon her performance in track. One would think the administrators would do everything they could to help her get that scholarship. But Dana and Staunton disagreed. I thought Dana wanted the glory of saying Jennifer was her athlete, that she had coached her into being one of state's finest.

Jennifer and her parents fought the move tooth and nail. I had coached her for a year, with phenomenal success, and she felt at home running with the boys. The principal, however, insisted, "There is a girls' coach, and it's not Anderson." The debate intensified, and the head coach of the girls' track team began to berate Jennifer. Jennifer's parents complained to both Staunton and the district administration that Jennifer had been injured many times before she came to the boys' program and that she had run without injury ever since. Above all, they said, the change might jeopardize her chances of receiving a scholarship to Stanford.

Both Staunton and the district's vice superintendent denied their request. Unable to be coached by me, and feeling that the girls' head track coach and the principal were harassing her, Jennifer transferred out of Huntington Beach. She never ran as fast again, and Stanford withdrew its scholarship offer.

Jennifer fell victim to a war of diseased adults unwilling to do what was best for her. She felt victimized by hatred and jealousy. In my journal I wrote:

> *I sit in denial. Could it be? I lost a part of my family, a part of my heart. Jennifer has my support and love. I just can't see not having her at the meets. Although she's only been with me a year, she's earned four years of respect. Her desire to pursue what was right for her intrigued me. Her talent amazed me. Her smile warmed me. I will miss her. Good-bye, Jenny. May the wind forever be at your back.*

## Track

We began the Duo's junior year in track looking as if we could be Huntington's best distance team ever. With Tony, Dan, Jess, Jake, and Jerryme, we had the strength and depth to excel not only in individual events but also in relay races. Strutzel was one of the top returning half-milers in the nation, and we expected him to break meet records all year long. Still, we were saddened at having lost Jennifer.

One afternoon early in the track season, a short, spirited runner from Westminster High School named Ronnie Alvarez came to practice looking for me. I was absent that day, so he asked

Harrison for my number and called me at home that evening. Ronnie, Westminster's top runner, said his team didn't have a coach and wanted to know if he could train with us during the track season. I told him he would first have to gain proper administrative approval from Westminster and then call me back. Ronnie phoned me the next evening.

"Hey, Coach. They won't let me train with you guys," he said.

"I'm sorry about that, Ronnie."

"You know what I'm thinking? I think I'm just going to transfer to run for you next year."

"Really?"

"Yeah. I don't even have a coach here."

"If that's the case," I said, "the first thing you need to do is call our vice principal, Darrell Stillwagon, and let him know. I'm not allowed to talk to you about it until you've contacted our administration."

"Tell you what, Coach," Ronnie said. "I'll come down to Huntington Beach tomorrow and tell him in person. That way I can pick up the forms while I'm there."

"Sounds good," I said. "We'll be at the track at 1:30. Once you've talked to Stillwagon, come see us."

"OK, Coach. See you tomorrow."

Ronnie's transferring would be great for us. Although he wouldn't actually be able to run with us until the summer, having him the next cross-country season would certainly help our team. We would have Tony, Dan, Jake, and now Ronnie. We still needed a solid fifth man, or we wouldn't be as good as last year's team. But we still could do well. A lot of it would depend on how much talent Ronnie had. His times were good—for running under poor coaching conditions—but not nearly as good as the other transfers.

The next afternoon Ronnie galloped across campus with paperwork in hand. Although I had never seen him before, I knew it was him; his large smile and jubilant presence matched his voice. I shook his hand and began to introduce him to the team. "This is Tony. He was Orange County Champion last year in cross-country and—"

Ronnie interrupted, "And he ran 14:52 at Central Park and ran 9:22 for the 3,200 as a sophomore in CIF where he placed second." Ronnie knew Tony's statistics better than I did.

"Yes," I said. "And this is Dan. He ran 9:58 as a freshman and—"

Again Ronnie intruded, "He ran 15:56 at Mt. Sac last cross-country season and 15:03 at Central Park."

"I see you know all about Dan too. What do you know about Jess?"

"Jess came to Huntington after winning the 800 county championship in 2:00 as a sophomore in track. After training with you, he ran 1:53 at Trabuco Hills and 1:51 in CIF. He almost beat Michael Grainville a few times." Ronnie continued, "And that's Jake Childs. He ran 9:49 in track last year. That's Jerryme Negrete. He came from Marina and ran 16:05 to be your fifth man when you won the Orange County championship last season with his 32nd-place finish."

After the team left for a warm-up, I talked to Ronnie about transferring. "Why do you want to come to Huntington Beach?" I asked.

"You guys are the best," said Ronnie. "I've been reading everything about you. I want to make a move for my senior year. I wanna go big time! Hell, we've never even won a dual meet at Westminster, Coach. I don't even know what it feels like to beat a *shitty* team. You guys at Huntington, you win everything. I want to win for a change."

Ronnie's hunger and desire were strong, but did he know? "Ronnie, are you aware that I'm gay?"

"Of course."

"Do your parents know I'm gay?"

"Yeah, my mom isn't cool with it, though. She's afraid you'll turn me gay. But my dad said, 'If that's where the best coach is, then he should go there.'"

"But your mom is willing to let you run for me?"

"Of course. Shit, my mom doesn't tell me what I can and can't do. Besides, my dad is excited. He's seen you guys kick ass."

"You sound like you'd do well on our team, but there's so much stuff going on here," I said. "You need to know that if you come here, it won't be all fun and games. I work my runners hard, but worse than that, if you come here, you're going to have a lot of enemies. When Jake came and when Jerryme came, even when Jess came, their old teammates gave them shit. They lost a lot of their friends. Are you willing to give up your friendships?"

"Coach, my friends want me to go. They know there's nothing at Westminster for me. They've been telling me to go to Huntington Beach for years."

"Do your friends know I'm gay? Because if they do, they're going to assume you are too."

"Hell, Coach, they don't care. In fact, one of them said you were his substitute a few years ago. He thought you were totally cool. My friends aren't like that. Besides, if they think I'm gay, oh well."

"That's great. I wish we all had friends like that. But once you're here you're going to be on the receiving end of a lot of crap. We aren't treated too well here. We get harassed, and the principal doesn't support us. After we won the Orange Country championship last season, he didn't even congratulate us. If you come here, you'll be in the middle of a lot of turmoil."

"I like that, Coach," Ronnie said. "It's like everyone knows who you are. I don't care what they think, as long as they all know me!"

"So you're prepared to be discriminated against?" I asked.

"I'm Mexican. I know what it's like."

"So you're prepared to be thought gay for transferring to our team?"

"I got my chicks. I'm not worried."

"Are you prepared to be called a fag dozens of times a day?"

"Hell, I'll laugh at them. I'll just say 'Whatever, dude.'"

"Are you prepared to have you car keyed?"

"Keyed? Is that all? At Westminster they get broken into and stolen."

"Are you prepared to go to meets and have other teams snicker at you?"

"Snicker? What's that?"

"Are you prepared to have them make fun of you?"

"All I'll say is, 'Who's got the trophy, baby?'"

A chuckle and a smile later, I said, "Welcome aboard."

Ronnie filled out the transfer papers, and they were approved. Soon after, he invited me to his house to meet his family. We talked in his living room, and Ronnie fascinated me with his knowledge about our team. Huntington Beach intrigued him so much that he had memorized everything he'd ever read about us. He knew about my training program and had even read my book.

Ronnie's dad broke into our conversation and said, "Show him your room, son."

Ronnie showed me the room he shared with his sister. Newspaper articles about Huntington Beach plastered every square inch of his half. I stood in disbelief. He had turned his room into a Huntington Beach shrine. He had saved newspaper articles that even I hadn't. He not only knew the names of my old athletes but also knew for which schools they were now running.

Ronnie's paperwork was accepted and processed. He would officially become part of Huntington Beach's distance-running legacy the following cross-country season and would begin training with us that summer.

Meanwhile, our team was busy winning everything in sight. And when the Arcadia Invitational rolled around this year, Jess, Dan, and Tony were all invited. Last year I'd had one runner, this year, three. From my journal:

*I am numb. I remember sitting in the bleachers of my first Arcadia meet in 1988. I dreamed of one day coaching a run-*

*ner good enough to make it. Doing so would mean I had one of the finest runners in the nation. Last year I got Jess into the 800. This year I go into the nation's premiere event with not one but three runners. I am trying to keep in mind that this season is fleeting. Jess and Jerryme have only a few races left with me, then it's the Duo's, Jake's, Simon's, Ronnie's, and my final year at Huntington Beach. Then I will be saying, "This is the last time I will run this meet."*

Everyone ran well at the Arcadia meet. Jess lost to Grainville again, but that was expected. My runners' times were so good that I decided to take them to the 97th running of the Penn relays, an event that showcases the finest relay teams in the nation. To get in, you must run a very fast qualifying time. We did and decided to go.

The trip began three hours after we'd beaten Fountain Valley in a dual meet. We drove straight from the meet to the airport, and six hours later we landed in Philadelphia. Knowing the memories of the trip would outlive the memories of just the race, I insisted we rent cars and drive the three hours to Washington, D.C. There we walked the presidents' and soldiers' memorials and toured Congress.

The next day, Friday, our group toured Philadelphia. It was great to have Tony and his parents, Dan and his parents, Jake and his parents, Jess and his parents, Jerryme, Harrison, Erich, and me all on vacation together. We first went to Independence Hall, where we viewed the Declaration of Independence. We learned about the crack in the Liberty Bell, saw Ben Franklin's grave, and then headed to the stadium to dig our own grave. For the first time in my coaching career, my team finished a race in second-to-last place. When your team is used to not only winning but also breaking records, second-to-last place is mortifying. We left the stadium the moment the race ended.

Back at the hotel I talked to each runner individually to determine why we'd run so poorly. We were fatigued from the travel and the pressure of the meet. My gut feeling was that we should skip our next race, scheduled to take place in a few hours. I wanted to drive to New York or Atlantic City, anywhere other than the stadium. The team members, however, decided they wanted to redeem themselves. So we ran again and we bombed again.

A trip to the Gettysburg Memorial helped us forget our Philadelphia flops. The park was packed with statues and hallowed history. We took a tour that ended with us sprinting up Little Round Top, just as the South had done. We drove back to our hotel late and flew home the next morning. We returned to California to answer that awful question: "How did you do?"

*       *       *

The dual meet season ended, and the championship rounds of competition went well. We swept most of the races in our league competition and launched into the series of five meets necessary to make it to the California state meet. Tony and Dan ran amazing times in the two-mile. Tony ran 9:12, and Dan ran 9:16. Unfortunately, Tony missed making it to the state meet exactly as Ben had, by just one spot. Jake and Jerryme both ran considerably faster than they had at their old schools. And Jess made it to the state meet again. It was a glorious race. Jess got a good start running in the fifth position for the first lap. On the third curve he noticed Grainville taking off. Jess wanted to pursue but was hindered by runners in front of him. When he hit the Strutzel Zone, with just 300 meters to go, he took off hard, pursuing Grainville. He began closing the gap as the crowds cheered. He moved into fourth, third, and then second place. He made ground on Grainville with just 100 meters to go. But the hard move cost Jess. With 50 meters left he began to falter. Grainville ran off with the victory, and another runner nipped Jess by less than a tenth of a second at the finish line. Nonetheless, it was a glorious third-place finish. He became my first, and only, California state meet medalist and was accepted to the school of his dreams, UCLA, on full scholarship. He and the nation's best-ever high school 800-meter runner Michael Grainville ended up running together for UCLA and became good friends. Jess would emerge as one of the nation's top collegiate 800-meter runners in the following years and is now planning to run in the Olympics.

Unfortunately, the graduation of Jess and Jerryme left the team with two big holes heading into my final year as a cross-country coach at Huntington Beach. We needed to fill both spots if we were going to make it to the cross-country state meet. I hoped Ronnie would be able to fill Jerryme's shoes, but we still needed one more outstanding runner. No talented new recruits were coming, and the deadline to transfer had already passed. The only way our team would be good enough to make it was if we found a runner from within our current roster. It didn't look good. Simon Bhavilai, the kid who'd introduced himself by saying, "I'm not very fast, but I really like to run," would have to be our answer.

Simon had worked hard for three years and had improved steadily. During the past track season he had established himself as an average varsity half-miler. At longer distances, however, he was not so good. If Simon were to help us, he would have to improve his three-mile time by more than two minutes. The average high-school runner improves only 35 seconds a year. Still, he was all we had.

# Chapter Seven

## The Negrete Incident

The day before graduation, the 1996 track season ended. Jess and Jerryme were graduating the next day, and the campus was abuzz with year-end festivities. I had not seen the seniors in a few days because they had dances, parties, and other activities to attend. But I looked forward to watching them graduate. After the ceremony I would meet them on the field and take photos with them in their caps and gowns. Jerryme planned to attend a trade school where he would learn how to repair cars. Jess would run for UCLA.

My pager buzzed while I was driving home. I looked at the number and recognized it as Jerryme Negrete's. It was followed by 911, which my athletes knew they should only use in emergencies. I opened my cell phone and dialed. A haggard voice answered. It was Jerryme's mother.

"Kathy?"

"Gumby?"

"Yes."

"Gumby, Jerryme has been beaten up."

The story has its roots in an incident that occurred nine months earlier. I had sent our runners into the locker room to change. We'd had a host of problems in the locker room at Huntington Beach, particularly with the football team. As mentioned earlier, the worst of the football players were the sophomores. To end some of the tensions, I moved the team to the varsity football locker room, where we had changed without serious incident. Most, but not all, of the varsity players were more mature than the sophomores.

At the beginning of this school year, however, when I sent the runners to change, one football player, Josh Spencer, decided that the distance runners were not allowed to enter the locker room. Josh blocked the entrance, proclaiming the locker room to be property of the football team. Jerryme, a young man with a temper, decided not to take such treatment and proceeded to enter. The football player shoved Jeremy, and a fight threatened to follow.

I was outside the locker room organizing materials in my van for the trip we were about to take to Las Vegas. On suspension at the time, I could only supervise. Jake came running from the locker room to find me. I sprinted across the parking lot, flew through the door to the locker room, and saw Jerryme and Josh posing as two titans awaiting battle.

"What the hell is going on?" I asked.

Jerryme and Josh continued to stare at each other, neither answering. One of the other football players said, "You guys are not allowed to change in here anymore."

"What?" I asked.

"This is our locker room. You guys can't use it."

"This locker room belongs to the school, not the football team."

"Our coach says no one else is allowed to use it. We're not supposed to let anyone in."

"What? Jerryme, Josh, Jake, you guys come with me," I said.

I pointed to another football player, "Go get Coach Pascoe and tell him to meet me in the principal's office. Now!"

We had already been pushed out of one locker room because of harassment. I wasn't about to cave in again. I asked Jerryme, Josh, and Darrell Stillwagon to sit. After telling the vice principal my account, he looked at the football player and said, "So what were you doing?"

"Coach Pascoe told us it was our locker room and not to let anybody else use it."

The football coach entered the room a few minutes later. He was annoyed that I had asked him to come to the meeting. "I'm in the middle of practice," he said in a surly tone.

"This is a little more important, George," I said.

Pascoe explained that the locker room had suffered damage by vandals during the summer, and the football booster club had paid to have it cleaned. Because of this, the coach had told his athletes to watch for others using it. But, he said, the players were not told to push people out.

"So let me see if I have this straight," I said. "We were moved out of the main locker room because the football players wouldn't stop harassing us. And even though I told the administration and Coach Pascoe several times what was going on, no football coach has ever supervised the locker room. Finally, we had to move to the upper locker room, which, again, the football team decides we can't use."

"It's not exactly like that, Eric," Pascoe said.

"Oh, it's not? So tell me what it is like."

"We just didn't want anyone else to use it so it wouldn't be messed up."

"And you thought the best approach was to give your athletes the responsibility of supervising it? Did it even occur to you to tell me in person or perhaps put a note in my mailbox?" I then looked to Darrell and said, "So if we can't change in the lower locker room

because the frosh/soph football team harasses us, and we can't
change in the upper locker room because the varsity football team
doesn't want us there, where can we change?"

Darrell said nothing.

To make matters worse, Josh, the football player, was notably
homophobic. I suspected he was "protecting" the locker room for
other reasons. He was one of the football players who had
expressed his hatred of homosexuals and harassed Erich when he
started the GSA.

In the end, Darrell decided to do nothing. He said he could not
punish the football player because a coach or a teacher hadn't witnessed
the incident. Darrell offered me the choice of either suspending both
boys for five days or suspending neither. This didn't make sense.
Punish Jerryme? For what? So I opted to suspend neither of them.

Josh left the meeting knowing he had gotten away with his
actions. No suspension, no detention, nothing. He was free to talk
it up. Knowing the nature of that player and the inability of the
administration to handle conflicts, I asked Darrell to write me an
account of the incident for my files. It read:

> *Tuesday, September 12, 1995, Darrell Stillwagon*
>
> *Josh Spencer (football), Jacob Childs (cross-country), and
> Jerryme Negrete (cross-country) had a confrontation in the
> football locker room. The cross-country team had been
> changing for practice in that locker room. The football play-
> ers were "protecting" what they felt was their locker room.*
>
> *Coach George Pascoe, Coach Eric Anderson, and I met
> with the involved students. It was agreed that the coaches
> would handle the situation with their respective teams.*

I couldn't believe so little action was taken over something
that was clearly only the tip of the iceberg. Matters began to

escalate a few days later. Josh sat a few seats away from Jake in their government class. Jake told me that Josh was bragging to his friends about his pushing the "fags" out of the locker room. I immediately reported the incident to Darrell, who grew irritated.

"What can we do about it?" he asked. "Kids will talk."

"Darrell, you have a problem here," I said. "This incident isn't over, and it's only going to get worse. You have a responsibility to protect the students at this school. *All* of them. How are you going to ensure my runners' safety in the locker room?"

The solution? A bathroom.

Darrell gave me the key to a bathroom. Our new locker room. We had moved from the main locker room to the smaller locker room to a bathroom. What next? A closet?

Despite my warnings, the situation between Josh and Jerryme was ignored. Had I been the administrator, I would have sent the athletes to conflict mediation, and I would have had a conference with both boys' parents. Furthermore, I would have mandated that the football and cross-country coach supervise the locker room daily. None of this occurred.

Nine months later my worst fears came to pass. Jerryme and a friend were driving home from graduation practice. Josh and two other football players pulled alongside. Somebody flipped somebody off, and a car chase ensued, the football players chasing Jerryme and his friend. Jerryme managed to evade them by driving through a residential neighborhood. They pulled in front of Jerryme's friend's house and went inside.

They remained inside for approximately five minutes before leaving the house to walk across the street to a neighbor's home, believing the chase had ended. As they crossed the street, Josh and his football friends rounded the corner, stopped the car in front of the house, and ran toward Jerryme. Josh ordered the other football players to hold back Jerryme's friend. To date, each side maintains the other threw the first punch. Jerryme and his friend swear Josh did. Josh and the football players claim it was Jerryme.

What happened next is indisputable and horrific. Josh tackled Jerryme and sat on him. He pounded Jerryme's face with closed fists. He fractured one side of Jerryme's jaw and continued to pulverize, breaking the other side while yelling, "I'm going to kill you, you fucking cross-country faggot!"

Josh continued the onslaught, yelling, "How does it feel to get fucked up the ass, you fucking faggot?" Jerryme tried desperately to cover his eyes as Josh scraped and gouged at them.

Jerryme's friend yelled for Josh to let up. "Stop it! Stop it! It's over! It's over, Josh!"

Josh screamed, "It ain't over till you're dead, faggot."

After a desperate struggle Jerryme managed to free himself of Josh's hold. His vision, bloodied from the beating, impeded him as he fled. Josh chased him, still enraged. Jerryme managed to scale a fence, and Josh, because of his size, was unable to follow. Jerryme ran home, where his mother placed ice on his face and called the Huntington Beach Police Department. Two officers came to interview Jerryme at his home. Unknown to the officers, Jerryme's dad was a retired cop. After the interview, Jerryme's dad was outraged. The police had classified the incident as "mutual combat."

"Mutual combat," I said. "You've got to be kidding."

"Not only that, but they didn't even want to know the names of the other kids involved," Kathy said. "My husband says they're just going to sweep it under the rug."

"This is more than a police matter," I said. "It's a school matter too. There's a law called *in loco parentis* that states the school is responsible for the welfare of students until they arrive home. Jerryme was on his way home from school when another student assaulted him. Call the school and inform them. If the police are sweeping it under the rug, call the paper."

She called both, and a few hours later I called Staunton to find out what was happening.

"At this point we're investigating it, Eric," he said in a clearly uncivil tone.

"Well, I'd like to know what's going on," I said, "since I need to know what to tell my kids and their parents."

"I'd tell them they have nothing to worry about."

I called Staunton back a few minutes later. "I have the *Los Angeles Times* on the other line right now," I said. "They want to interview me. I told them I couldn't talk to them until I had spoken with you."

"I'd be very careful about you say to the paper," Staunton said.

The next morning the following article, accompanied by a picture of Jerryme's bruised and battered face, appeared on the front page of the Metro section of the *Los Angeles Times*:

> Huntington Beach—A cross-country runner from Huntington Beach High School says he was beaten by another student athlete who shattered his jaw while calling him a "faggot," possibly because the runner's coach is openly gay.
>
> Coach Eric Anderson said Tuesday's incident appears to be the latest harassment suffered by the school's cross-country runners since he announced his sexual orientation to students and staff in 1993. "We had people throw a bottle at us," Anderson said. "We had kids drive by while we were running and call us fags. We had kids in class called fags." Huntington Beach detectives said Wednesday they are investigating the complaint by 18-year-old Jerryme Negrete, who alleged he was attacked by a 16-year-old football player who repeatedly called him a faggot while pummeling his head. No charges have been filed.

Huntington Beach High School Principal Jim Staunton said he interviewed the football player and characterized the incident as a fight between two teens. Staunton described the football player as an "excellent student who scored 1,300 on his SAT test." The principal questioned whether the coach has an "agenda" and is inappropriately portraying the incident as homophobic.

"Our immediate intent was to get to the guys who were supposedly the victims of an assault," said Staunton, who said he reviewed written statements from Negrete and a friend who was with him during the incident. "This doesn't look like an assault. I think what we have is a fight."

The two youths had a previous locker room confrontation last fall, the principal said. According to the football player, Negrete used foul language on Tuesday and threw the first punch, splitting his lip, before the 16-year-old made antigay comments, Staunton said.

But Negrete told police that the 16-year-old and two other teens tried to pick a fight Tuesday afternoon while driving alongside Negrete and a friend as they returned from graduation practice, Huntington Beach Police Lt. Dan Johnson said. The football player and his friends then showed up at the home of Negrete's friend and attacked Negrete, the runner told police. The teen said the 16-year-old repeatedly called him a "faggot" and made crude sexual remarks while beating him.

I said, "No, I'm not gay." Negrete said Wednesday, his voice muffled by swelling. "He was punching me on the side of the head. I couldn't get up because I was trapped on the ground."

Negrete is scheduled to undergo surgery Friday to repair and wire his shattered jaw. Family members said he delayed the surgery until then so that he could attend his high school graduation today.

Negrete's mother, Kathleen Negrete, said her son and his friends on the cross-country team have spoken repeatedly of the antigay harassment they have faced since Anderson went public.

"This is a problem," she said. "It's been a problem, and it will continue to be a problem unless the school takes strong action."

Coach Anderson, who knows of no other openly gay high school coach in California, said the incident underscores the often homophobic atmosphere of school athletics.

Staunton said there were prior incidents of antigay taunts against cross-country runners two years ago but that the main culprit was a student who has since graduated and was told that "he shouldn't do that."

"I do not see, by any means, a widespread problem," Staunton said. "To say that there is no problem would be naive, but to say it is any kind of widespread problem? No."

The principal said school officials have worked with the Orange County Human Relations Commission this year to address issues of ethnic tension and intolerance.

Anderson said that his runners experienced "dozens" of incidents of harassment after his public disclosure but that "this year has been vastly improved."

The coach said he decided to come out to school officials and students three years ago because he suffered from ulcers and migraines and was "miserable" from hiding his sexual orientation.

Anderson, 28, said his openness prompted "volumes of kids" isolated by their sexual orientation to come out to him and tell him that they too are gay. The year Anderson came out, a student gay and lesbian support group called the Student Alliance also formed on the Huntington Beach High School campus.

But his announcement also prompted some parent complaints and "a rise in verbal assaults against my runners," Anderson said. "I would bring the complaints to the administration."

Anderson said he never expected his team would be targeted because of him. He said he had only heard Negrete's version of Tuesday's events but that it seemed to fit a history of taunts experienced by his runners.

Negrete said he and his teammates have nothing but respect for Anderson, who has coached at the school for 11 years and is known by the nickname Gumby. The youth said his team is upset with school officials for not doing more.

"I think it's wrong, and I think it's fine to have a gay coach on campus," Negrete said.

Furious, I read the comments Staunton had made and decided to head to the school. Tired of playing nice, tired of fearing Staunton, I intended to find him and berate him in front of as many people as I could.

I arrived at the school, parked the car, slammed the door, and trudged across the quad in search of Staunton. I had never scolded him before, never even raised my voice. I spotted Staunton entering a building and headed toward him. David VanHoorbeck, our athletic director, stopped me. "Did you read the article this morning?" I asked.

"Yes, I did," he said.

"Agenda? I'll tell you what my fucking agenda is! I want peace for my team!"

Just then, Staunton appeared. He exited a classroom and walked away from it. He caught my eye, stopped, looked at me, and then turned away with his head hung low.

"I'm going to have it out with him," I told David. "I can't believe what he said!"

"Eric, do you know that Darrell Stillwagon died this morning?"

"What?"

"He had a heart attack."

"Oh, my God, no."

Staunton walked away.

David began to cry. I felt too enraged to cry and too distraught to rage. Not knowing what to do or say, I walked back to my car.

I left the scene and drove to work. I walked through the front doors and sat at my desk. My fellow teachers said nothing to me. They knew nothing of Darrell's death, and they assumed I would be in a tirade over the newspaper article. I set my briefcase down, pulled out a stack of papers, and opened an answer key to grade them. Then, without warning, I burst into tears.

Two teachers approached. One put her hands on my back and said, "He's an asshole, Eric. Everyone who reads the article will know that," she said.

"Darrell died," I said.

Darrell Stillwagon had died just three days before his retirement.

That afternoon I attended a solemn graduation ceremony. News vans surrounded the school. The death of an immensely popular administrator on graduation day deserved such attention. Darrell's shadow hung over the ceremony. It was the first time I chose not go to the field after the ceremony to take photographs with my graduating seniors. I was too depressed to be cheerful for them. Besides, Jerryme was not very photogenic after his beating, and I didn't know what to say to him. So I waited by the exit for my athletes to leave, where a group of reporters had also gathered.

I stood, waiting for the seniors to exit, leaning against a fence. A reporter stopped a student who turned and pointed at me.

"Coach, will you talk to us?"

"Has there been a lot of harassment?" the reporter asked. "How long have you been out?" The reporters were not there for Darrell's story but for Jerryme's. I gave a couple of interviews.

I returned to work the next morning and a secretary said to me, "Tricia Savage phoned from NBC. She wants you to call her."

This was it, my chance to go for the throat. A story on national television would be the ultimate way to expose Staunton. It would bring national attention to our plight. I had in my hands the phone number to deal a terminal blow to my nemesis. He deserved it. He had failed to protect us, had harassed me, had failed to recognize my athletes' achievements, and had tried to prevent me from gaining employment. He had messed with me way too often.

I began to dial but didn't finish.

Perhaps I did this in memory of Darrell. Perhaps I didn't want to kick a man when he was down. Or perhaps I just wanted to return to my coaching. I don't know why I hung up, but I did.

Whatever the reason, I refused future interviews, refused to speak with the Orange County news channel, refused NBC, and even refused CNN. I'd had enough.

Staunton did not escape as easily. Two news stations ran stories that night. A few days later the *Orange County Weekly* shredded Staunton with a front-cover story. *The Advocate, Out,* and several local gay publications ran articles too. The school was flooded with calls of complaints, and I received dozens of calls of support. People were outraged.

"This doesn't look like an assault."

"A 1,300 SAT."

"The coach has an agenda."

Staunton's own words would bring him down. I didn't need to say anything. Jerryme had surgery the day after his graduation. For the rest of his life, he will have five screws attached to his lower jawbone.

A few days later I received a call from Staunton. He updated me on the situation and then asked if I would attend the Orange County Human Relations Committee mediation program with him. I thought this was not an idea of his own design; someone higher up the chain must have told him to do this. Nonetheless, I agreed to go.

On July 9, 1996, I met with Staunton and a mediator. The plan was to open up a line of communication and map out a gay-sensitivity training program for our campus during the following school year. We struck an agreement in the meeting, deciding that I would stop by his office from time to time to tell him how the team was doing, and he would make the effort to go talk with the boys and find out how they were. I told him I would bring problems straight to him, and he agreed to do what he could to solve them. In short, we agreed to disagree on our past and to try to make my final year at Huntington Beach peaceful for all.

After the surge of media attention, Jerryme's surgery, and the beginning of summer, things died down. Our new freshmen arrived, and I gave them the standard "Welcome, we need you, we are fun, we are good, there are no cuts, but this is a hard sport" speech. I had one year left. We had one final season to pursue my ultimate, and elusive, goal of making it as a team to the state meet in cross-country. Then it would all be over.

# Chapter Eight

## The Duo's Senior Year

*Cross-country*

Qualifying for the state meet would not be easy for us this year. We had five senior runners: Tony, Dan, Jake, Ronnie, and Simon, but overall they were not as good as the previous year's team. Having Dan and Tony up front would help, but how much better can you do than first and second place? I expected them to improve and to lower their personal records, but their improvement was not likely to help us lower our team score. Jake's placings would certainly improve over last year, but would Ronnie even be as good as Jake was last year?

Then there was our fifth man, Simon. He had a lot of pressure on him. In cross-country if your top runner has a bad day, he might fall from first to fifth and lose four points. But if your fifth man has a bad day, he might fall from 40th to 70th and cost the team 30 points. Therefore, in a sense, the fifth man is in many ways more important than the first.

During the summer I became Simon's training partner, just as he had done for Jennifer. He became the object of an intense improvement effort. This tested my abilities as a coach and his as an athlete. I talked him through countless workouts, guiding him, instructing him, giving him faith. He steadily improved throughout the summer.

I had to do more than train Simon to run the times; I had to train him to handle the pressure of performing. The variable of pressure destroys many top runners. It takes years of competitive running to learn to handle it well, and Simon had little experience with it.

Attempting to sensitize Simon to the extreme pressure he would experience as our fifth man, I began putting pressure on him as early as the last track season. In several relay races I entered him as our team's anchor, the king of all pressure positions. Other coaches thought I was crazy for putting our weakest runner in the anchor leg, but I was preparing him for our next cross-country season. Simon did well only a few times. His attitude, however, was excellent. He would run himself into the ground for us. He wanted to excel, to share in the fame of our other runners. Moreover, he wanted to help me achieve my final goal.

Not a day of summer training went by without Simon hearing, "Come on, do it for the team." During every 15-mile flat and easy run, he visualized himself effortlessly passing hordes of runners in the state qualifiers race. And when we raced to the top of Mt. Baldy, which we did every Memorial Day, he climbed the 10,064-foot mountain faster than Jerryme Negrete had the previous year. Simon began to keep up with the rest of the team in select workouts, and by summer's end he was outrunning *me*. The team grew excited at his improvement. Ronnie, especially, took interest in helping Simon.

As the season drew nearer, I mapped out our strategy, deciding to break our season into thirds. In the first three invitationals we would experiment, train through, and not worry how we placed. The next three races we would take more seriously, and in the final three we would go for victory. I revealed the plan to the team during our usual Monday meeting. When Ronnie heard me talking about training through the first few meets he lashed out, "Hell, no, Coach. I want to win everything!"

"You want to win everything, Ronnie?"

"Hell, yeah. That's why I came here, Coach. You guys win everything."

"All right, then. We will take Thursdays and Fridays easy. We will rest up for each invitational. We will, Ronnie, win everything."

"That's what I'm talking about, Coach," Ronnie said with a wide smile.

### Victory Number One: The Las Vegas Invitational

The air was characteristically dry and hot in Vegas. We had come to claim the title for the fourth year in a row. Our white jerseys, sporting HB on the front and our names on the back, were familiar to the Nevada schools. The gun sounded, and we took to the middle of the pack, just as planned.

I had created a default plan of racing from the middle of the pack, which allowed Jake to run with Tony and Dan for a longer period of time. Running with teammates is easier and would help Jake place higher. Ronnie was especially strong at coming from behind during the last mile, so Simon could run with Ronnie for the first two. The only runners who didn't gain an advantage from going slowly at first were our front runners, Tony and Dan. So during some races I'd ask them to hold back and help Jake, and during others I'd say, "Run away with it, boys."

The race went as planned. In the final mile Dan broke away from the pack with stunning strength. He left Tony behind and blazed a new course record. Tony came in third, Jake 11th, Ronnie 17th, and then we waited for Simon.

This was Simon's first test, and he performed beautifully. He finished only a few places behind Ronnie.

When Ronnie came through the other side of the finish chute, I told him we had won. He hugged me and then danced about hugging his teammates, exclaiming, "Yeah, we won it baby! We won it." Ronnie's happiness put a smile on my game-day face; it taught me something too. Watching Ronnie celebrate reminded me of how happy such victories used to make me. I vowed to enjoy this final season to the utmost, to appreciate even the smallest victories.

That night, during our traditional postrace celebration I raised my soda glass to toast our triumphant team. "To Dan. To his individual victory and to his new course record. To Simon, our new hero, who improved so much that he ran a minute and 47 seconds faster than his personal record. Finally, to Ronnie, and his first-ever team victory. Gentlemen, we're going to have an awesome year!"

## Victory Number Two: The Edison Dual Meet

No sour grapes this year. We ran full force and beat them easily.

## Victory Number Three: The Dana Hills Invitational

The Dana Hills Invitational gathered a collection of more than 40 top-notch teams. The race came as a relief for Tony, as he had not been running well. His summer event times—such as the 12-hour relay, which we again won and for which we set a new course record, and the Mt. Baldy eight-mile uphill run—were slower than they had been the previous year. At the Las Vegas Invitational Dan had left Tony as if he were standing still, and although the team won the race, Tony ran slower than he had the year before. Things weren't looking good for the defending county champion. At the Dana Hills Invitational, however, Tony changed all that. He and Dan tied at the finish line with an awesome time of 15:09. The race reminded me of their freshman year, when they often crossed the finish line together.

As a team we not only won the invitational but also had combined individual finish times faster than any in the history of Huntington Beach High School. Jake, Ronnie, and Simon all ran personal records, and our team began to catch the attention of the press.

Before the season started, most people assumed Huntington Beach would be strong up front with Tony, Dan, and Jake, but that we'd have no one else. Ronnie's transfer hadn't drawn attention because no one had heard of him. But after a summer with our team, he was a runner to be reckoned with. Then, of course, people asked me, "Where did you get that Simon Bhavilai?"

## Victory Number Four: The Fountain Valley Dual Meet

Jake easily ran away with the dual meet victory against Fountain Valley. After the hard time Fountain Valley gave us about his transferring to run for us, Jake liked to rub our success in their faces whenever he could. Tony and Dan paced Jake for three miles, and then allowed him to win in an impressive 15:46.

## Victory Number Five: The Marina Dual Meet

An easy victory.

## Victory Number Six: The Stanford Invitational

Stanford, one of the most competitive races in the nation, provides a good preview of the California state meet. This year more than 40 teams were entered. We ran horribly; our runners were sluggish and mechanical.

At the end of the race I was upset. For the life of me I couldn't figure out why we ran so poorly. As each runner came out of the finish chute, I gave him explicit directions to warm down alone and to provide an answer as to why we ran so poorly. By warming down alone, runners are less likely to attribute their poor performances to reasons supplied by other runners. I can hear what each athlete thinks for himself, and can tally their uninfluenced opinions. Upon returning each runner said, "No idea, Coach. I just couldn't go."

In what I thought was a bad joke, Tony and Dan came running over to me about 20 minutes later and said, "Coach, we won."

"Not funny, Tony," I said.

"No, Coach, we really did."

"What?"

Dan confirmed it, "Yes, Coach. We won. The results have been posted."

"It must be a mistake. We didn't win. We got pulverized!"

The results proved them correct; we had won.

I had never thought we could win the Stanford Invitational. The competition was so good, in fact, that this was only the second time I had brought the team. The previous year we had finished sixth, and I thought that was damn good, considering we were up against many of the best teams in the nation. First place? When we'd run so poorly? I was stunned.

As time passed, I grew happier about our victory at Stanford but was still concerned that we had run so slowly. The team was doing well, though. We now had beaten 91 teams. The quality of competition, however, would get tougher as the season progressed. I wanted desperately to win another Orange County championship and to qualify for the state meet. If we didn't improve, we wouldn't meet these goals.

## Victory Number Seven: The Los Alamitos Dual Meet

The dual meet was an easy win but not a self-esteem builder, especially for Tony. Dan and Jake ran away with the victory, but

Tony lagged behind, losing to a runner from Los Alamitos. We played it off as if Tony was just taking it easy, but I knew that wasn't the case. In addition to Tony's not running well, all of our times were slow. It seemed the team was actually losing ground. I was frustrated.

Jake's dad jabbed an elbow into me. "Coach," he said, "what are you complaining about? You guys are undefeated. Hell, it's getting kind of boring winning all the time." It was true. We did win the race, and we had not lost one yet. I sat the team in a semicircle and addressed them.

"OK, guys, congratulations on another easy victory," I began. "We are now 92-0. It's nice to win all the time, isn't it? The first half of the season is now over. Competition will grow fiercer as other teams improve. We have not improved in the past two weeks. In fact, I think we have lost ground. I can't figure out why we ran such slow times at Stanford and today. Maybe I've over-trained you. I don't know.

"It's nice to win when we're not at our best, but I want us to be at our best from now on. If we take the week off, maybe we'll run faster next Saturday at the Central Park Invitational. So we're going to take five days off starting tomorrow."

### Victory Number Eight: The Central Park Invitational

"A truly marvelous performance!"
"Just what the doctor ordered!"
"See, all we needed was some rest."
"Boys, now I know we're ready to win county again."
We ran magnificently at the Central Park Invitational, which falls just one week before the county championships. Dan and Tony ran together in the middle of the front pack until their traditional breakaway point when they took over the lead and ran away with the victory. Ronnie, Jake, and Simon all ran inspiring

races. Ronnie and Simon both had improved so much that even other coaches congratulated me on their performances. We were now 137–0, and it looked as though we would repeat as county champions the next week.

I spent the majority of Sunday preparing team and individual strategies for the county championship meet. As I had the year before, I gathered the stack of statistics I had compiled over the season for each competing team. I broke the top teams down into their individual runners, charted those runners' performances, tracked their histories of performance under pressure, and did the same for our team. I worked out another complex strategy for our team, which used individual efforts within to help us repeat. The feat would not be easy since the quality of competition was greater this year than the year before. Fortunately, our team was better now than it had been last year, something I definitely had not expected.

It took me several hours to complete the strategy we would employ over a 16-minute race. I planned to deliver the strategy in a meeting on Monday afternoon, in my weekly team address. On Monday morning, however, I received terrible news.

David VanHoorbeck, our athletic director, called me. "Eric, we have problems."

"Why? What's up, Dave?"

"There's a form, a blue form, that I didn't file with the CIF."

"What kind of form?"

"One that Ronnie turned in last spring as part of his transfer papers."

"So?"

"I just discovered it on the bottom of a stack of papers. I was supposed to turn it into the CIF months ago. Transfer students are not eligible to participate in sports until that form is filled out."

"What does this mean?"

"Ronnie is not eligible to run until the form is completed and approved by the CIF governing body."

"So let's get it approved," I said.

"For the CIF to process the form," he said, "Westminster has to sign it, and they have refused."

"On what grounds?"

"They're claiming you recruited Ronnie illegally."

Larry Roth, the Westminster athletic director, strongly opposed the transferring of athletes for athletic purposes. He was irate that Ronnie had transferred to run for Huntington Beach and therefore refused to sign the necessary form. Rules dictated he could refuse only on grounds of illegal recruiting, an accusation with which I was all too familiar.

"We'll fight the charge," David said. "But it could take longer than a week." Until then, Ronnie cannot train or race with the team. I'm sorry to tell you this, but it gets worse."

"Worse?"

"Because Ronnie was ineligible when he raced, you'll have to forfeit all the races he has run."

"What? That's every race!"

"I'm sorry, Eric. It gets worse."

"Worse?"

"The dual meets will now count as losses, and that will statistically damage your chances of making it out of league competition."

"I can't believe this."

"Staunton wants to speak to you as soon as possible," David said.

"Tell him I'll be there at noon."

That afternoon, an hour before practice, I knocked on Staunton's door. This time the situation was not about his trying to get me; rather, it was one we both abhorred. Staunton expressed his belief in my innocence and his dismay that Westminster was acting in such a petty fashion.

"I'll have to follow procedures for this matter," he said. "It starts with questioning you and then Ronnie."

"That's fine. Let's begin," I said.

"Did you ever talk to Ronnie about transferring?"

"No."

"Did you ever train Ronnie illegally?"

"No."

"Did you ever…"

"No, no, no."

"OK," Jim said. "I need to talk to Ronnie about the charges. Once I've done that, we can begin to fight. Why don't you talk to him first, explain the situation, then bring him to see me at 1:30."

At 1 o'clock my runners gathered in our meeting room. I opened the door to find my jubilant teens doing what they did every day at this time: talking loudly, throwing Skittles at each other, and laughing. Every Monday I went over the training schedule and race strategies for the upcoming week. Today my runners were eager to discuss my plan for winning another county title.

"Tell us the plan, Coach."

"Yeah, Coach, how are we going to repeat?"

Ronnie shouted, "Orange County champions, baby!"

Jake took notice of my long face. "Quiet down, guys! What's wrong, Coach?"

I took a deep breath. "Gentlemen, I have some bad news."

My once joyous runners came to a sudden hush as they focused on what I said. "I hope to one day forget this speech," I began. "This has been a season of dreams for us. I'm extremely proud of how well we've run. Simon, your improvement, and Ronnie, your improvement, have been glorious." I paused. "When Ronnie transferred to Huntington Beach, he did everything properly. He turned all the forms in on time. But one of the forms was not processed." I looked at Ronnie. "I am so sorry, but you have been ineligible all season long. We have to forfeit our victories."

Ronnie spoke up, "No! No! That's bullshit. I turned in every-thing. I did everything right! I checked with Stillwagon a dozen times. What the hell is going on?"

Dan began to cry.

"It gets worse," I said. "Not only do we have to forfeit every race we've won this season, but Westminster is pressing illegal recruiting charges. Until that has been cleared up, Ronnie won't be able to run or train with us. We're going to try to get him cleared by Saturday, but it doesn't look good. If he's not cleared in time for the league meet, he won't be eligible to run in CIF, and our season will be over."

My athletes quickly spun from denial to anger.

"This is fucked, Coach," Simon exclaimed. "They did this on purpose. You know damn well Staunton is behind this."

"He's not," I said. "I don't believe this was done on purpose. This makes the administration look bad too. I honestly believe this was an oversight. David VanHoorbeck is very upset and will be here at 1:20 to speak to you personally. At 1:30, Ronnie, you have an appointment with Staunton."

Soon after, VanHoorbeck came in to make his apologies. He was short on words, obviously distraught. He took full responsibility for the error and said the press release would reflect this. He left after the apology, leaving the team in shell shock.

"We're just going to have to move on from this, guys," Jake said. "We have to get Ronnie eligible and pick up where we left off."

"This is bullshit!" Simon exclaimed. "I swear they did this on purpose."

"No way," Jake said. "The athletic director just screwed up. Staunton might do that to us, but VanHoorbeck wouldn't. Look, man, he felt horrible about it. He screwed up. It's done. I think we should forgive him."

The boys walked out to the football field and pulled David aside. Jake said, "Mr. VanHoorbeck, we want to let you know we understand this was an accident and that we forgive you." David's eyes misted. "Thank you, boys. You're very mature and deserve better than this," he said. "I will fight to get Ronnie eligible, I promise."

After Ronnie talked to the principal, the rest of the team walked into Staunton's office and expressed the same sentiments they had for VanHoorbeck. Staunton was moved. I guess he figured that since they were my kids, they would look at this as a reason to berate an administration that had not backed them in the past. To blame the administration, to cry foul, he knew, would have been a perfectly reasonable reaction.

Yet the boys held no animosity. They accepted the situation as simple human error. And then, like true heroes, they focused on what they could do. Their mature behavior did something for Staunton. He took charge on our behalf.

Staunton asked to speak to me alone for a moment. "I support you 100% on this," he said. " I believe everything you've said, and I want you to know I was touched by the civil manner in which you and your boys handled the situation with David. I will do everything I can to get Ronnie cleared as soon as possible. I'm waiting for a call from the Westminster principal right now."

"Thanks, Jim. I'm going to take the guys on a run, but I'll stop by after the workout."

"I'll be here," he said. "Just make sure Ronnie doesn't run with the team until he's cleared. We don't want to give them anything else to use against us."

After our 15-mile run, which Ronnie ran alone, I returned to Staunton's office to see how his conversation with the Westminster principal had gone. "She refuses to sign the form upon the recommendation of her athletic director," Jim said. "The next step will be to contact the CIF and find out what to do. Hal Harkman, the CIF official, was out today, but he'll be back tomorrow. I'm hoping we can get him cleared by county championships on Saturday. But if Westminster is making charges, they'll have to be dealt with, and these things take time."

The following morning, Tuesday, Staunton phoned to say he had arranged for David and me to go to Westminster that afternoon to talk with their athletic director, vice principal, track coach, and principal. He then faxed me a copy of a letter the Westminster track coach had drawn up regarding his allegations of my illegally recruiting Ronnie. The allegations were an amazing fabrication. The letter was mostly about how Ronnie had "lied to the track coach" at Westminster and how I should punish Ronnie for being "immature" at Westminster by not allowing him to run at Huntington.

I took letters written by Paul Wood and by the girls' cross-country coach and my assistant coach, all stating that Ronnie had not trained with us before his transfer, that he had made first contact. Still, Westminster refused to sign the form.

After returning from the meeting, Staunton grew incensed that they would withhold Ronnie's eligibility on the grounds of undue influence without actually saying what that influence was or when it had occurred. On Wednesday, Staunton spoke to the vice superintendent of our district who, upon hearing the story, said he would sign the form in place of the Westminster principal. I was talking to Ronnie in my office when Staunton called to tell me we were in the clear. I hung up the phone and hugged him. "We're in the clear, Ronnie! Tomorrow morning I'll take the day off work and drive to see the vice superintendent. He'll sign the form in place of the Westminster Principal, and then I'll drive to CIF myself to have it approved."

I woke early the next morning to take the form to the vice superintendent. When I arrived, however, he had changed his mind, saying we would have to meet with the principals in the district to determine whether Ronnie had been illegally recruited. The next scheduled meeting wasn't until Monday afternoon, two days after the county championship meet.

I returned to Huntington Beach to tell Staunton, who was again outraged. He made a call to the vice superintendent, who happened to be one of his best friends, and had it out with him. He hung up the phone in anger. "I'm sorry," Staunton said. "He's talked to Westminster and thinks there may be something to the charges. He wants to do things properly and have a hearing."

Up, down, up, down…down. I left Staunton's office with news that Ronnie would definitely not be eligible to run in the county championships on Saturday. We would not repeat as county champions. I pulled Ronnie out of his English class to break the news. Ronnie cried. There was nothing I could do.

I delivered the news to the team. "If they rule in our favor, we'll get Ronnie back in time for our final dual meet and our league finals race. Listen, gentlemen, this is serious. Because we had to forfeit our other league races, we now have a 0–4 league record. The way the system works, we will have to beat Esperanza in the dual meet and then win the league meet as well. Otherwise, we won't place in the top three in our league, and we won't go to CIF. Do not underestimate Esperanza's abilities. They're ranked sixth in the county, and we're racing on their course, which has 47 turns. Earlier in the season the entire Marina team went the wrong way and was disqualified. The Esperanza dual meet is only five days after the county championship. I want to be well-rested for the dual meet against Esperanza on Thursday, so if you feel tired during Saturday's race, back down and go easy."

## The Orange County Championships

We announced that Ronnie was sick and would not be running. I feared the truth might bring a flood of people calling to testify that they too saw Ronnie train with us illegally or that "Gumby tried to recruit one of my runners too." False accusations like this would only serve to compound the matter. So Ronnie had the flu that day.

The race wasn't good for us. Although we tried to put the week of stress behind us, its effects were clear. Tony and Dan ran poorly, way out of the running for the individual title. As a team we ended up in eighth place. Truth is, I think we were more concerned with the outcome of Monday's meeting.

Principal Staunton came to watch the team run the county championships for his first time ever. We gave him an honorary Huntington Beach cross-country sweatshirt and cap. He ran along the course, cheering for our team. In the end, he was amazed at the positive environment of the cross-country team and pleased that we had finished as well as we had. When the race was over, I walked him to his car and had the most pleasant conversation I had ever had with him.

Six principals, the vice superintendents, and both athletic directors attended the meeting to determine Ronnie's eligibility. I arrived nervous; Ronnie, in fact, was more confident than I. We walked through the district office doors and were forced to wait in the same room as Larry Roth, the Westminster athletic director who had sworn revenge at Ronnie. I was impressed that Ronnie made the first gesture to shake his hand. I followed suit, though I had little desire to show him respect.

The panel first asked to speak with Ronnie. They questioned him for 15 minutes and then called me into the room. I sat at the end of the table and answered questions regarding the circumstances under which Ronnie had come to Huntington Beach. Their questions were designed to find a discrepancy in our stories. There were six schools in our district, and it would take four to vote Ronnie ineligible. I feared a vote of retaliation by the district principals. I feared that Fountain Valley, Marina, and Westminster might vote against us because they had each lost an athlete to us. Edison might be the swing vote but might vote against us because we had elected not to run our best athletes in a dual meet against its team. Or perhaps the principals wouldn't care much about those situations and would vote based on the facts and not out of retaliation. Not knowing, I nervously answered the principals' questions. They dismissed me, discussed the issue, and voted in closed session.

The vice superintendent emerged from the meeting. "Go home," he said. "Your principal will let you know the decision in the morning."

I had been prepared for a verdict. I wanted this misery to end. I saw the rationale of not telling us while all parties were still in the same room, but why not let us find out later that day?

I called Staunton that evening. "I thought you might call," he said. "I just sat down to a glass of wine, but I'm sworn to secrecy until 8 o'clock tomorrow morning. I'll call you at work. For now, just hang in there."

I called 15 people, asking each, "Do you think a glass of wine means he's celebrating or that he's drowning his sorrows?"

At 7:55 A.M. the phone rang.

"Congratulations, Eric. Ronnie's eligible," Staunton announced.

It was over. The nightmare was over. We would have Ronnie, and with him we could pick up the trail leading to the state meet. I paged Tony with the code we had agreed meant Ronnie was eligible. When I opened the meeting room door that afternoon, I found a collection of jubilant faces.

Earlier that day I had made a bogus appointment to speak with Staunton. His secretary told him he had a meeting scheduled with a city council member. In reality, I had assembled the team in the principal's office, and when Staunton opened the door we surprised him with a thank-you reception. I broke out several bottles of sparkling apple cider, and Jake and Ronnie each gave a speech in gratitude. We then presented him with a thank-you card signed by each member of the team and the coaches.

After the celebration, I had a private talk with Staunton.

"Jim, I wanted to thank you in person. You fought for us, and I appreciate it. It's nice to be on the same side for once."

He said few words, but they were significant. "I've learned a lot, Eric. Perhaps something good did come out of all of this."

### Victory Number Nine: The Esperanza Dual Meet

We were forced to forfeit our previous dual meets even though we had won them all, and now we had just one dual meet left. The opposing team, Esperanza, was our toughest competition in the league. To advance to the state qualifying rounds, we had to win this meet and then our league championship meet. If we lost the dual meet or placed second in the league meet, we were done for.

The entire running community had its eyes on this meet. The newspaper touted it as "the fate of Huntington Beach," saying, "The two top ranked teams in the Sunset League will battle it out today. Huntington Beach, who was forced to forfeit..."

Anxiety on the starting line was high.

We couldn't have any screwing around today. I had planned that at the sound of the gun, Dan, Tony, and Jake would run away from the field. In a dual meet a first-, second-, and third-place finish is statistically an automatic win. They had to place one, two, and three because it was possible that all seven of Esperanza's runners were faster than Simon. If we didn't place one, two, and three, we would likely lose the race.

Tony and Dan would pace Jake. They both could easily beat every Esperanza runner, but it would be much more difficult for Jake. Two of Esperanza's runners had beaten Jake earlier in the season. With Tony and Dan pacing Jake, they could encourage him each step of the way; they could break the wind for him and keep him fresh.

As the gun sounded, a nervous crew of parents, coaches, and teammates awaited the outcome of the dual meet that would determine the rest of our season. Dan and Tony took to the lead, sandwiching Jake between them. By the mile mark the trio had broken away. Esperanza's coach began to furiously yell at his runners, "Stay with them, damn it! Beat Childs or we'll lose!"

Winning or losing this meet made no difference to Esperanza. Statistically, they had already won the league title since we'd had to forfeit our previous wins. Beating us today would only keep us from competing in the championship rounds. Had the roles been reversed, I would have bowed my head to the other coach and instructed my athletes to run easy to make sure the other team won, but this was not Esperanza's style.

Esperanza's coach wanted us to lose. He marked the course with arrows supported on stakes to chart the way through what could only be called a labyrinth. The arrows were small, and an approaching runner would have to slow at each of the 40-something curves to see which way to turn. This was not a problem for his athletes, who trained on the course weekly, but it was a serious handicap for ours. Knowing Esperanza's coach as I did, we had driven to the course earlier in the week to make sure we knew it without the aid of his arrows.

Ronnie, now a legal runner, ran in seventh place at the mile mark. By the two-mile mark it was obvious my boys were going to place first, second, and third, and I breathed a sigh of relief. It looked as if we would make it through this first hurdle. Meanwhile, Ronnie worked his way through the ranks, and with a half a mile to go, he moved into fifth place.

Fans from both teams crowded the finish line. Dan rounded the corner in first, closely followed by Tony in second, and Jake in third. Then came a runner from Esperanza with Ronnie attacking from behind. In a last-minute blaze of glory, Ronnie outkicked the Esperanza runner. We placed first, second, third, and fourth!

### Victory Number Ten: Sunset League Finals

A first-place finish in our six-team league would provide us with a ticket into the CIF preliminaries. A second-place finish would end our season. Confidence was high, as we had destroyed Esperanza, the toughest team in our league, in the dual meet just a week earlier. We planned not only to run away with the meet but also to ensure that everyone who read the results in the paper knew Huntington Beach was back and was kicking ass. We may have had the worst official record in Huntington Beach history, but we were undoubtedly the best team the school had ever had.

When the gun sounded, no one had a hope in the world of beating us. Dan won the race, Tony placed second, Jake seventh, Ronnie 11th, and Simon 13th. No one came close to beating us. Huntington Beach was back and ready for CIF action.

## CIF Preliminaries

To make it out of the CIF preliminaries, we would have to place in the top four of 12 teams present. The teams were all good, but I believed we were better than everyone, except Righetti. Tony and Dan ran the first mile too hard but managed to finish third and fourth. Jake, however, ran a phenomenal race, coming from 30th place at the mile mark to sixth in the end. Ronnie ran what I considered the best race of his career, despite falling and rolling down one of the hills. With blood running down his leg, he got up and finished the race. He stayed with Jake almost the entire way and finished an impressive eighth. Simon's 37th place was too far back for us to beat Righetti, but it was a good race for him. We finished second and would run in the state preliminaries the following week.

Two other races were to take place that day, each of which would send four teams to the state preliminaries, making a total of 12 teams. After our race I stood on the finish line and took notes on what the other teams were doing. Scary. That was the only way to describe the quality of the other teams. In total, seven schools ran better than we did. This meant we were ranked eighth going into the state qualifying race, and two other teams were right on our heels. Only four teams would qualify for the state meet. I had some serious strategizing to do. The course was like running in the

Himalayas, and our team was good on hills but not good enough. All seven schools ranked in front of us were situated in the hills, and since Huntington Beach is not exactly hilly, they had a huge advantage over us.

On Sunday I devised a complex come-from-behind game plan. I spent an hour explaining it to the team on Monday. On Tuesday the five-day forecast warned of possible weekend rain. If it were to rain, the course might be changed to a flat one since muddy hills are dangerous. A flat course would give us a better chance of qualifying for the state meet. But even if the course were flat, we would still face a formidable challenge.

On Wednesday, just three days before the race, the forecast for rain was more certain. So I abandoned our old strategy and created one for the rain course. A flat course, I thought, means everyone will be overly excited and will go out way too hard. My gears spun.

"Gentlemen, here's the plan," I began at our Thursday afternoon meeting. "We'll come from behind. We'll have extreme patience the first mile, taking to the very back of the pack if we need to. We'll arrive early, measure out the one-fourth-, one-half-, and three-fourths-mile marks. We'll make sure to run on pace the first mile, paying no attention to what the other teams are doing. I suspect they'll go out way too hard, and we'll let them. After the mile mark we'll begin to work our way up. The rain course will only allow me to see you three times: at the three-fourths-mile mark, the mile mark, and the 2.5-mile mark. You'll have to run off your own faith in your pacing.

"Individually, Tony and Dan, you'll need to place in the top eight. Jake and Ronnie, you both have to place in the top 20. Simon, you have to place in the top 70. If you do, gentlemen, I think we'll qualify. Pressure will be high, higher than you've ever experienced. But if we do everything in the manner we always do, we stand a good shot at making it. We'll arrive early, warm up together, and stretch with our usual partners." I ended with, "Let's pray for rain."

That night, the skies opened. It rained all day Friday. On Friday afternoon I called to see if our course had been decided. I called at 4:50, just ten minutes before the office closed at 5 o'clock. The secretary informed me that a CIF official had driven out to the course to determine if it was runable but wasn't expected back soon. The office closed at 5 o'clock, so we wouldn't find out which course we would be running until the following morning.

On a whim I called back at 4:58. The official had just returned, and he told me we would be running the rain course.

### Last Chance: The State Qualifiers

I warmed the team up properly this year. Knowing that I had corrected last year's mistake, we jogged, laughed, and enjoyed the spirit of doing things correctly. The dark skies brightened our spirits. The hills, which worked against us, had been flattened. The playing field was now even, and we were in the running. After stretching and lacing up our racing flats, the announcer called the runners to the starting line. I turned to our team and said, "Make me proud, boys."

While Erich, Harrison, and I jogged to the first viewing point at the three-fourths-mile mark, I reflected on how fast the year had gone, how fast all my coaching years had gone. One year earlier I had made the biggest coaching error of my life, thinking it had cost me our only opportunity for the state meet. Today I was being given another chance. I did everything right this time. If we qualified or not, at least I knew I had done my best.

We heard the gun sound from afar. The first three-fourths of a mile were run on a straight road. Over several minutes, we watched the herd of bodies grow. Finally, the leaders came close enough to be recognized.

*Come on, Dan. Come on, Tony. Where are you guys?* Finally, Dan emerged. He looked good, running in about tenth place. "Run the plan, Dan," I yelled.

*Where's Tony? Come on, Tony, where are you? Too many runners are going by. Did I miss him?* Then Tony appeared; he was in 20th, too far back. *That's OK. Maybe they're just running their pace. Maybe the others all went out too fast. Just wait and see where Jake is… Where* is *Jake?* He was in 60th. Ronnie was in 81st, and the only two runners Simon was beating were our sixth and seventh runners. Our team was dead last.

As I ran to the mile mark, I hoped that perhaps the plan was actually working. Perhaps the entire field except for us had gone out way too fast. It sure didn't seem that way. I yelled to my athletes to run their pace, regardless of what others were doing. I told them that if they did this, they would come out strong in the end.

After the runners passed, we took a tangent to the mile mark.

The team had made no progress in that quarter-mile. Nonetheless I yelled, "Have faith in the plan. Have faith in your abilities. You will move up! You will do it!" But our team was still in last place, and I began to think we were going to bomb. We wouldn't see the runners again until they were just a half-mile from the finish. Much would have to happen between now and then. I ran, sweating from anxiety. *Please let them have faith. Let them pass hordes of runners with pride. Please, boys, emerge in position.*

I was so overcome with anxiety that I began to cry while I ran. I arrived at the final cheering point, the 2.5-mile mark, and waited. I tried to hide my tears from Harrison and Erich, who said little. What could they say other than, "That was a stupid-ass come-from-behind plan, Gumby"? So they said nothing.

Harrison peered through his telescopic camera lens, trying to spot the runners' approach.

"I see green, blue, red…and white," he said. "Dan's in fourth place, Gums."

"Do you see Tony?" I asked

"No. Sorry. Wait. Yes. Yes. There's Tony. He's in eighth place!"

"Yes!" I exclaimed. "How far off the pack is he?"

"He's not. In fact, he's in seventh now."

Soon the lead pack approached. Erich and I yelled with all our might, "Yes, Dan! Yes! Go for second, Dan! Go for second! You can do it, Dan. You can do it!"

Then we cheered for Tony, "Go get that group, Tony! Go get 'em! Pull some in for us! Move up, Tony. Move up!"

Then they were gone.

Now to wait for Jake and Ronnie.

Harrison counted off the runners, "20, 21, 22…" We needed Jake and Ronnie to place in the top 20. "Twenty-eight, 29, 30, there's Jake. And it looks like Ronnie is right behind him." This was disappointing, since we were now 24 points behind what I thought we needed to qualify.

And then Harrison yelled, "Holy shit!"

"What? What's wrong?"

"Simon is with them!"

"*Simon?* You're kidding!"

"No, Gumby. It's Simon. He's right behind them!"

The pack flew by. We frantically cheered.

"Go, Jake. Go, Ronnie. Get up there. You can do it! Go boys!"

"Way to go, Simon!"

I yelled, "Simon, way to go! You're our hero, Simon! Go get five more men for the team, Simon!" I ran alongside him to get in a few more words of encouragement.

"Just get five men more and we'll go to state! Catch five men and we'll qualify! Do it for the team, Simon!" He soon moved too far out of range to hear me. After Simon passed, we hurried to the finish. Sweat streamed down my face, and my hands shook in excitement.

I arrived at the finish area to find a swarm of fatigued runners already gathered. I spotted Dan on the other side of a fence that kept me out of reach. "What place?" I yelled to him.

Dan held up one finger. He'd won!

Then Tony came into view, "What place?" I yelled.

Tony held up two fingers! I couldn't believe it.

Jake, Ronnie, and Simon soon crossed the finish line. They had held their positions. We qualified.

The team dog-piled one another. Harrison, Erich, the parents, and I broke out in hugs and cheers.

I had now reached all four of my goals as a coach: to advance an athlete to the state meet in track, to advance an athlete to the state meet in cross-country, to win an Orange County championship in cross-country, and to advance a team to the state meet in cross-country.

The team went on to finish sixth in the state championship meet. Tony and Dan established themselves as All-State runners. Jake and Ronnie got the victories and the glory they had wanted so badly from Huntington Beach, and Simon became a hero.

*     *     *

Before I close, I must tell one more story.

As my runners began their cooldown, moments after the announcement that we'd qualified for the state meet, a reporter interrupted me. The interview took a few minutes, and afterward I ran to catch my heroes. I didn't know that in those few moments something dreadful had occurred.

As my runners jogged their cooldown, a couple of boys from another school yelled, "Gumby is a faggot!"

Simon replied, "What?"

"Your coach is a fucking faggot, man!"

My runners had just qualified for the state meet. They had just run the best race of their lives. Now they were being harassed in their moment of glory. They advanced toward the other team prepared to do battle.